# LADY SEC

Beryl Blackman.

# LADY SECURITY

## SUE JONES

BANKHOUSE

First published in the United Kingdom in 2013 by

Bank House Books

PO Box 3

New Romney

TN29 9WJ UK

www.bankhousebooks.com

British Library Cataloguing in Publication Data
A catalogue record for this book is available from the British Library

ISBN 9780957305854

Typesetting and origination by Bank House Books

*To 'The Lads'*

# CONTENTS

## ACKNOWLEDGEMENTS:

Special thanks to my children who at times must have thought they had a part-time mother, and both of whom said, 'Just don't put us in the book' – sorry about that!

Thanks to Jan for a lifetime of support, laughter, and endless memories of beaches, mountains, weather reports, and of course Canada.

To Lofty Wiseman, Pete Scholey, Dennis Martin, Phil and Carol Jones and Rod Cooper – it was a real honour to know, train and work with you.

I'd also like to thank all those whose enthusiasm for the book took me completely by surprise. All the lads I had the privilege of working with (and if I've got you mixed up in different locations and at different times, I apologise now!); Shaun Criscuolo and Nana Kodjoe who kept me sane in London; Dave Conway, Boyd Fullerton, Julian Kilkenny and Colette Brannan, who kept me sane in Liverpool; John Hayward, Paul Gaskell and Chris Pilkington for their loyalty in Manchester; and Geraldine Robertson for pushing me in the right direction at the right time. Thanks should also be given to those who helped with the preparation of the book, but who didn't want me to put their names in. Thank you anyway!

And last but not least, to Bill – for always having my back covered!

## PROLOGUE

*L*ess than ten minutes ago the lift lobby on the tenth floor of the hotel had been deserted, the silence exaggerated because the lifts had been pre-programmed not to stop at this level. For the next two weeks no guest would set foot on this floor, with the exception of those with security clearance. The whole floor was to remain isolated and locked off from the rest of the hotel, with alarms fitted to all external doors and fire escapes. Only competitors, officials and security team members of the 1986 Miss World Competition could enter or leave.

Several women drifted into the lobby and I moved to take up my usual position, close to the dark-haired young female who draped herself elegantly across a settee placed there solely for such use. She gave me a cursory smile, then turned to talk to the equally beautiful blonde girl next to her. I knew the blonde only as Miss Sweden. The darker-haired young lady was Miss Israel; I was her bodyguard, and her safety was my responsibility for the duration of the competition.

Within a short period of time the lift lobby filled up with many young ladies, all beautiful, all competitors, and all chattering and laughing. I watched as several members of the Close Protection Team came into the area, including Pete Scholey, the ex-22 SAS veteran whose zany sense of humour had earned him the nickname The Joker during his years with the regiment. Within a few minutes he had all the girls doubled up in fits of laughter as he imitated them, us, competition officials and anyone else he could think of. The guy was a natural comic, a genius at impersonation.

The relaxed atmosphere was shattered by a sudden scream from one of the girls, and I immediately closed the distance between Miss Israel and me, looking for the threat and the reason for the cry. The girl concerned was on her feet, her hand holding a delicate strap attached at one end to her dress, the other end floating freely – a broken dress strap obviously a major incident. Her eyes flew round the now silent space until they met mine. A look of relief flooded her face, and she called, 'Oh, Lady Security, Lady Security, you fix.' It wasn't so much a question as a demand. Pity I didn't carry needle and thread. But two things stuck thereafter: that I was no more able to fix articles of clothing than my male counterparts, and that my name for the duration of the competition was Lady Security. The name stayed with me for many years afterwards.

# CHAPTER ONE
# GHOSTS AND DEMONS

**M**ost people have periods in their lives when they look back and wish they'd handled things differently, or been smarter, or stronger; or even wish that certain events hadn't happened at all. Hindsight is, of course, a wonderful thing. I was lucky with my life, because it was hectic bordering at times on manic, full of variety, and I didn't have time to stop and look back to see what mess I'd made along the way. I didn't have to; I had a legion of phantoms who constantly reminded me of my misdemeanours and failings. I'd called them my ghosts and demons, and throughout my career they'd presented me with memories of events or incidents I'd handled or experienced. Actually, they didn't just remind me, they haunted me until I dealt with the memory and moved on. They were like chapters in a book, sometimes following a plot, and sometimes completely random.

Ghosts that followed me out of close protection were fewer and more serious than the ghosts that followed me out of hotels. When I worked as a bodyguard I believed, as I believe now, that a contract, once accepted, became a bond of silence. Clients were entitled to privacy, so memories stayed memories and loyalty kept them silent, unless that contract had operated in the public domain. Then I believed I was entitled to discuss certain aspects of the role; after all, it had already been viewed by an interested populace. Anyway, some things are better not discussed than discussed and not believed! That is probably why I'll always be happier talking about hotels – they are an open stage, and everyone within them is an actor; they ooze drama!

There were many ghosts along the way, but no more than half a dozen demons. Most of these evaporated over the years, leaving only one that disturbed me. In fact it wasn't really my demon; it belonged to someone else. I just inherited it, and probably wasn't meant to keep it. It was like a hot potato – drop it fast or pass it on. But I hadn't done either; I'd kept it, believing it to be my responsibility until confrontation day. Even thinking of the incident I heard the report of a shotgun and smelt cordite.

*The field looks wide, with few trees and a good clear panoramic view. The two men with me carry their guns locked and loaded. In my opinion this makes them both idiots; I don't want one of them slipping and accidentally discharging either gun in my direction. I promise myself I won't be doing this again. As we climb over the fence I make sure they are in front of me, and neither muzzle is pointing in my direction. On the other side of the fence I see that the field hides several deep depressions that could easily conceal a grown man. I change my opinion about the suitability of it as an ideal place for clay pigeon shooting. I like to have a completely uninterrupted view before I pull a trigger. But the land we're shooting on belongs to one of the men, is deep in the Welsh mountains, and is not the sort of terrain you'd pick for an afternoon stroll. The traps are in place, and it doesn't take long to set them up with clays. I've shot with both men before, but always in another location. This site gives the opportunity for 'blind' shooting, with the shooter never sure when or where the clay will come from. We take it in turns loading and releasing the clays: it's a good afternoon, and I enjoy the practice. At the end of the afternoon one of them informs me that in a couple of days he's 'off on duty' for six months or so, and will have to wait a while before shooting again. He suggests that I continue to go shooting with his colleague while he's away, but I know I won't be taking him up on the offer. I don't know either man particularly well; they just turned up at the club one night, and began training with me. Within a couple of weeks I found out we had mutual friends in the security field, enjoyed firearms practice, and shortly afterwards began shooting together.*

*We walk back to my vehicle and I give them a lift back to the farm. Driving home, I wonder where his line of duty will take him. He told me once that his career took off in the Royal Navy, and he'd 'gone on from there'. I hadn't asked any more, and he hadn't told me. When I get out of the car and unlock the boot to get my kit out, I notice a brown paper package tucked into the corner. My naval colleague had it with him when I'd picked him up earlier in the day. Before we went shooting he'd put it in the boot, saying 'Don't let me forget to pick this up afterwards, will you?' 'No, of course not,' I'd replied; but it looks as if we both forgot. I pick it up, but apart from the wrapping there's nothing else on it. It feels like a stack of papers. I put it back in the boot, go into the house and ring his number. When there's no answer I debate briefly whether or not to take it back to him, but he lives over an hour away, and I'm longing for a long, leisurely soak in a hot bath. I guess he'll phone me soon enough when he realises he's left it. But he doesn't phone, and when I don't get an answer the following morning I drive over to his farm, cursing him all the way. I'm surprised to find the entire place locked up.*

He never did contact me about the papers, and in fact I never heard from him again. For a long time I never knew what those papers were. That discovery was the birth of a demon.

## CHAPTER TWO
# INJUSTICE

I faced most forms of crisis during my thirty-five year career; from assassination attempts, shootings, stabbings, suicides and hotel fires, to bomb and terrorist threat, and I thrived on them. But the things I struggled most with throughout my line of work were incidents of disloyalty and injustice. Now I'm no heroine in flowing robes with a sword in one hand and a set of scales in the other, but nothing was guaranteed to wind me up more than the feeling that justice had not been carried out or disloyalty had gone unpunished. When it meant that someone working in my own line of work had betrayed trust or confidences, it was like a red rag to the proverbial bull, and I was off on a rampage. I never did learn to control it.

One of the most bizarre incidents I ever dealt with involved a triangle of disloyalty, injustice and betrayal. It happened when I worked in a Manchester hotel – actually it happened shortly after I left that hotel, but I got caught up in it anyway. It started right out of the blue, raged for months, and disappeared as quickly as it had arisen, leaving me feeling that not only was it one of the strangest incidents I'd dealt with, but also one of the most frustrating. Even more exasperating, I had been left with the sense that I would never find out exactly what had happened. Surprising really, because the incident involved a world-famous footballer and his wife, whose lives were continually played out via the media circus. It had certainly shocked me at the time, turning into an extremely long and complicated affair that left a bitter taste after it was apparently all over.

Just thinking about it made the ghosts swirl, and one of them tapped me on the shoulder and scathingly whispered, 'Not as clear as you first thought, was it?'; and every detail replayed itself.

*Malta: September 2008. I'm on holiday, and trying very hard to relax. It's been many years since I've last been here, and this time around I'm not working, am weapon-free, and determined to enjoy the leisurely Mediterranean life.*

*It's never good when your mobile rings in the middle of the night, not in my line of work anyway. I roll over and look at the small screen. It shows 'Hotel 3'. This is strange, because the title belongs to an ex-colleague who works in a top hotel in Manchester – a hotel I'd left several months earlier. We'd used call-signs for professional reasons and for clarity of communication. I'd been Hotel 1, Bill Foster, my second, had been Hotel 2 and our night security officer was Hotel 3. As far as I'm concerned there is no reason for him to be ringing me, but before I can answer it the phone falls silent.*

*Bill is with me in Malta. When he joined the team it quickly became obvious we would get on well together. We had the same sense of humour, and the same attitude and approach to security. It had been a great working relationship: platonic and professional. We'd shared the same interests, a passion for Canada, wildlife and the outdoors, and after I left the hotel we spent several holidays travelling in Alberta together. Despite both being happy with our own company, it was probably inevitable that after Canadian winters and log cabins, we'd end up sharing a flat in Manchester. There wasn't an ounce of romance in either of us, but it had worked, and it suited us both.*

*I turn over, listening to Bill muttering something rude about phone calls in the middle of the night before carrying on snoring. I want to ignore the call completely; whatever the problem is, it can't be mine. But* some things you can't change, and whether or not I like it I know I'm going to return the call. For Hotel 3's sake I hope it will be worth the cost of a call to the UK.

I dial the number and wait for it to ring; but the call won't connect, so I eventually decide that it must be a mistake or a misdial, and go back to sleep. How wrong can I be?

Two weeks later we're back in the UK in a Costa coffee shop in Manchester, sitting in front of the person who made that call. 'Sitting' might not be the right word: I'm leaning forward, mouth open, probably looking stupid. Bill has just spent a couple of hours with Hotel 3, so has already gone through the stunned expression bit. He sits quietly opposite, watching my reactions.

'He put what in the footballer's bedroom?' I didn't really need to ask the question, because I'd heard perfectly clearly the first time. 'Was his wife with him?'

Hotel 3 nods and carries on with his story.

'Covert cameras. Bedroom and living room.' He holds my gaze, and I find myself believing him.

'Why?' I ask, immediately realising it's a silly question. 'He would have been taking an awful risk. Their team could have carried out a sweep.'

I look over to Bill, who's worked with the footballer's security team more than I have. He raises his eyebrows and shrugs, as if to say, 'Well, you and I would have.'

'You're 100 per cent sure?' I say, my mind running through all the implications.

'Yes. So sure I took pictures.'

'What, you took pictures, of covert pictures he'd taken of the bedroom?' I'm aware I'm starting to sound a bit incredulous.

'Yes, pictures of the equipment he used, and pictures of the pictures on the screen on his equipment. It showed everything very clearly.'

Hotel 3 takes a deep breath as if he is about to explain something to someone who is very slow at grasping things.

'I was working nights, and they were in-house,' he continues. 'The security manager, let's call him X, decided to stay over in the hotel, even *though the couple had their full security team staying. He'd booked a room for himself next to theirs. We now know why. I thought at the time, stupid sod, they have a top security team working for them, and he's conceited enough to think his presence in the room next to theirs is necessary. He wouldn't have known what to do if something did "kick off". He breaks off to laugh, slightly bitterly. 'Anyway, I'd borrowed X's master key to get in somewhere, I can't remember where and it doesn't matter, and he'd radioed me to meet him outside his room and bring the key back. When I got there he wasn't in the corridor and he didn't answer the door, so I radioed him again – but he didn't answer that either. In the end I used his master key to open the door, so I could put the key on the table next to his bed. I didn't think he'd mind because we were so busy that night. That's when I saw all the equipment. It shocked me, I can tell you. I mean, cameras, listening gear ...'*

'What?! He was listening to them as well?'

'Yes, he had this screen with pictures of the suite showing the bedroom and living room, and there were wires attached to listening gear. It freaked me out.'

I know exactly what he means, because the whole thing is starting to freak me out.

'Go on', I say, 'what did you do?'

'I took pictures of it all with my mobile phone.'

I sit back in my chair, the beginnings of doubt creeping into my mind. 'So you had time to take pictures? Weren't you worried he'd come back and catch you?'

'Yes I was, but I thought if he came back I'd be able to challenge him. He shouldn't have been doing it.'

'So why not just challenge him anyway?' I ask, beginning to feel a bit dubious about the whole thing.

'I wanted proof. I knew nobody would believe me.'

'Go on. What happened next?'

'Nothing. I took the pictures, left the key for him, left the room and got on with what I had to do. I was supposed to be dealing with a guest as well, and she was already getting impatient, and ...'

I stop him in mid-flow. 'You left the key in his room ... wasn't that a bit stupid? I mean, you've more or less told the guy you've seen what he was doing.'

He shrugs his shoulders. 'At the time I was planning to tell someone, but both of you had left; I couldn't trust many others. I was going to show you guys and ask what you thought I should do. Then, later, when I did try to get hold of you, you were abroad.'

'So nothing else happened?'

'Oh yes, it did. About ten minutes later I got a phone call from him. He asked me if I'd been in his room, and I said I had, and he said we'd better get together to discuss it.' He stops, looking past me as if trying to recall the details of the conversation.

'Well? What else did he say?'

'Nothing. That was the strange thing. I said I couldn't meet him because I was busy, and he repeated that we needed to discuss it, and I said I didn't know what he was talking about.'

'And that was it?'

'For the time being, yes.'

I look at him again. 'You're going to have to forgive me, but this is so unlikely and so serious, it's a bit difficult to believe, never mind think of the consequences.'

Hotel 3 laughs. 'I thought you'd say that. I also thought at the time that I was in deep trouble, which now we know I was – well, am! They suspended me for theft shortly afterwards don't forget. He had connections with the police, he'd been a police officer, his wife was supposedly a police officer. I thought I had to protect what I had.'

'Go on. What did you do?'

'I sent a copy of the phone clip to my father in America. He's a barrister.'

'Yes, I remember. You told me once. But this is all so weird, and so hard to believe. If any rumour or leak of such a story got loose it could destroy the reputation of the hotel, possibly the entire hotel chain.'

I pause to consider the whole situation. If what he's telling me is true, it's such an unbelievable breach of trust and confidence that my head is reeling with the possible consequences.

*Hotel 3 is absently stirring his coffee.*

'Carry on,' I prompt him. 'You sent a copy to your father. It showed the pictures of the suite they were staying in, and the phone gave the date and time of the pictures. It was clear enough to be able to identify what was being filmed?'

'Yes.'

'Do you still have a copy on your phone?'

'Yes.'

'Then keep it safe, because if what you say is true this could cause untold mayhem. If the press get even a sniff of it they'll be after you and the hotel.'

'The hotel's already after me.'

'No. It appears only he's after you. In fairness to the hotel, if you haven't told anyone what you've got they're going to be as shocked as I am.' I think for a while before continuing. 'You know you should be talking to the hotel, and possibly the police, don't you?'

A look of anger comes over his face. 'After the way the hotel's treated me? I had the police come to my house and search it because they said I'd taken a pair of jeans and £30. I was set up; they never found anything. Why would I want a pair of someone else's jeans?'

I look at the designer clothes he's wearing, the sort of designer clothing I've always seen him wear, and can't answer.

'I told the police that I had information about why he would want me arrested. That he had a personal grudge.'

'Then why didn't you tell them exactly what happened?' I ask, perplexed. 'It could all have been sorted then and there.'

'I didn't tell them because of the way they treated me,' he continues, his face a mask of anger. 'They searched my house, locked me in a cell, a really filthy cell, they told me to remove my clothing and put me in some sort of disgusting, dirty, boiler suit thing. They did all that, but they hadn't even arrested me – and they actually never formally arrested me. They treated me more like a murderer than someone they were investigating over the loss of a pair of cheap jeans. I bet if they'd taken the time to call the guest who'd reported his trousers missing they'd probably discover he found them after he left. That always happens, you know that.'

I nod. What he was saying is true. Hotels regularly have guests who accuse the maid or room service of stealing something, only to find it once they get home. It's a common occurrence. Days can be wasted investigating, interviewing staff, playing back CCTV footage, carrying out lock reads and writing reports, only to have the guest find the item or, worse still, say that they don't want to take the matter any further. This inevitably means they've found it.

I interrupt again. 'I don't think they can do all that without officially arresting you. I'm sure they can't lock you in a cell without you having been arrested. It's taking your liberty away.' But I pause, not completely sure of the facts. 'Look,' I continue. 'You have to speak to someone. For goodness sake, they have heads of state staying in that room. God, the prime minister stayed there. If the recording equipment's still in place ...' I stop, because it really doesn't bear thinking about.

But Hotel 3 isn't listening to me. 'The only reason those charges were made was because he knew what I'd seen. He wanted me gone. He knew I'd caught him taking covert photographs of possibly the most famous couple in the world while they were staying in their suite. Hell, he had to get rid of me.' Hotel 3 is getting so worked up that people around us are beginning to stare. 'I've never had anyone slur my character like that. My father's advising me now, and I'm not dropping this until I get an apology from X, an apology from the hotel and an apology from the police.'

I look at my watch, knowing I have to get back to work and that Bill has to get to a meeting the other side of Manchester.

I try again as we stand to leave. 'You know, you really should speak to someone with a lot more clout and knowledge than I have. You have information about something that could affect powerful and influential people.' My mind conjures up a list of the VIPs from across the world who are regular guests. 'I'm not just talking about this couple, although that's serious enough. You need to speak to someone higher up in the hotel chain.' I name a couple of people.

A stubborn look crosses his face. 'No, that's not going to happen. I've never been treated like this before. When I get justice and apologies, then

*I'll let people know. Anyway, it's not just him. I think the general manager knew about the recordings; they'd been friends before that hotel, you know: they'd worked together in the past.'*

*As we part company I know there isn't much else I can say. He's made his mind up. But walking back to work I can't help but wonder if what he has told me is true – and what I should do about it, if anything. Part of me wants to protect the hotel, even though I haven't worked there for two years. But as Hotel 3 pointed out, this is now a police investigation and I shouldn't be getting involved – an amusing comment after all he's just told me! So I do nothing.*

*A few weeks after our last meeting with Hotel 3 I receive a phone call from an ex-colleague who is linked to the hotel. A request has been made for a security company to check the hotel for signs of any illegal covert surveillance being carried out. I ask where the search will take place, and the reply is that it's to be focused on the General Manager's office and the main suite. I get a second call a couple of days later informing me that the result of the search is positive.*

*Months later I'm interested to hear from an ex-colleague that the security manager named by Hotel 3 has gone on holiday and has never returned, a black mark apparently hovering over his name – but no-one knows what for.*

I pulled away from the ghosts, or they'd bog me down all day.

After our original meeting we met Hotel 3 several times; he said he wanted to bring us up to date. He always stressed that no-one ever charged him with theft, and to my knowledge he never would be. Things just moved slowly but steadily towards his unchanging goal. He wanted revenge, and that very much concerned me.

One of our last meetings had been short but worrying. He was still a very angry young man. All charges against him had been dropped by the police, which, if everything he'd told me was true, was hardly surprising. He'd always said that once charges were dropped and he was completely exonerated of any wrongdoing he would start to get his own back. He informed me that he'd launched official complaints against both the police and the general manager of the hotel. He also informed me that he was considering a job offer in the Middle East, completely fed up with the UK and its legal system. I didn't blame him for that. My own experiences with our legal system, and courts in general, had always left me drained and confused as to just whom the Crown Prosecution Service and courts support and deliver justice to. I understood why our courts were called Courts of Law and not Courts of Justice. Justice never seemed to come into it.

As I'd walked back to work after speaking to him that day, I thought about the hundreds of other incidents I'd been caught up in and the hundreds of people I'd met while working in hotels. Some had been famous, some had been high risk, some had just been everyday people hoping to enjoy a stay in a luxury hotel. I wondered if they had any idea of the reality behind it all: the crazy, frantic goings on behind the five star frontage and lip gloss smiles. The trouble with working in hotels was that you either loved them or you hated them: there was no in-between. Once you got bitten by the hotel bug it was difficult to move on, even though the work brought with it extreme levels of frustration, stupidity and arrogance, with aggression and violence thrown in for good measure. But for all that, I had suddenly known that the hotel I worked in then would be my last. Ten years really was enough.

I only saw Hotel 3 once more. He told me a senior police officer had been in touch with him, and from what he said it seemed likely that because of gross mishandling by the original police officers they were now facing disciplinary proceedings. There was something else bothering him, but at the time I didn't push him. Perhaps I should have done. A few weeks later, with no message or warning of any kind, and for no apparent reason, he completely and utterly disappeared. He has never been in touch since, and we have never been able to contact him.

As I said at the beginning, it was one of the most bizarre incidents I ever dealt with.

# CHAPTER THREE
# EARLY DAYS AND QUESTIONS

I moved into hotels by accident. That I remained working in them for ten years was more a reflection of their fascinating residents than the enjoyment of working in an environment where guests were gods and staff were replaceable! Before hotels I had a history of over twenty-five years in the field of personal security, ten of those as a bodyguard working in close protection. I had trained and worked with the best.

I think I was born to protect. Growing up between two athletic and outgoing brothers I probably had good reason to worry, and in doing so took my first steps into protection. Both my brothers loved motor bikes, and aged seventeen my elder brother's most prized possession was a Triumph Bonneville, on which he happily 'topped the ton' if an open stretch of road presented itself (with me as pillion if I could persuade him to take me). Both were accomplished athletes, long-distance runners, and my younger brother in particular would regularly lope off on his own, leaving me to imagine all sorts of accidents or injuries that might befall him while he was out without any form of communication. I always thought it was best to be with them so I could protect them; quite ridiculous really, because they were both taller and stronger than I was, and anyway, neither of them wanted me tagging along to spoil their fun. So, as I could neither run as fast nor for as long as either of them, and was too short for my legs to support motorbikes once they'd stopped, I had to be content with waiting, and planning what I would do if either of them failed to return. It served me well in later life.

As my brothers seemed more interested in fitness campaigns and lethal motorbikes, not to mention producing homemade fireworks in the outdoor shed (which resulted in at least two visits to the local hospital), and as my father, a master mariner, spent a large proportion of his time at sea, I believed this left me in charge of family safety and defence. I knew my mother was more than capable of this, but even she needed some support now and again. I was delusional I suppose, but this was the start of my interest in protection.

Years later I found myself regularly asked if I thought it unusual for a woman to be working in the field of security. I never used to think so, because I'd been planning all my life for the unexpected. But throughout my career the questions remained, and I was repeatedly asked the same two: 'Isn't it odd to find a woman doing this sort of job?' and 'How on earth did you get into security, being female?'

My reply was always, 'Oh, you know, you drift into these things, don't you?' But in reality I knew I hadn't drifted at all. I'd chosen my career because I was a born planner, with a love of the unexpected, a natural suspicion of anyone and everyone, and a fascination with conflict. Once, during a high-profile visit to a hotel that involved round-the-clock security, I was asked the now tedious two questions so often by high-ranking police officers that it got boring. But I found myself thinking backwards in an attempt to gain clear and definitive answers. Was it odd for a woman to want to work in security? How had I really started? When did I move from professional worrier to professional protector? Most people who work in the security field have a background in the military, martial arts or club doors. They've usually finished one career and are searching for another, either for financial reasons or because the first job wasn't fulfilling or challenging enough. So where did I fit in? The problem was, once I'd thought about the questions I had to find the answers, because when I really thought about them, really, deeply, I wasn't sure I knew the answers.

So I sent my mind off down memory lane on a quest to find out. Days later it came back with the negative thought that there was a lot of complicated stuff in there, all stored in random order, and unless I started opening some tightly closed boxes I'd probably never sort it out. Not having the time for all this opening and sifting (and possibly being lazy), I thought of those closest to me. Surely they'd remember, probably better than I did, what started me off on the security road. So I turned to them for help.

When I asked my mother if she could remember when I first became interested in security, she said, 'Goodness knows. It was a miracle you were born at all. Just before you were born I had to have an emergency appendectomy, and they told me I'd probably lose the baby. The elderly lady in the bed next to me said, "If it's a girl she'll survive." You were a girl, and you survived!'

This was fascinating and, I have to be honest, a little embarrassing. I didn't like the thought of anyone peering at me in the womb while I was unable to defend myself! But there were further revelations. 'You were a twin,' my mother continued. 'Unfortunately the second baby didn't develop.'

'What, there were two of me?'

'Scary, isn't it?' replied my mother, with an expression I couldn't quite determine.

Of course, I couldn't leave this information alone. I mean, if a chance question about the origins of my career could uncover that I'd once had a twin, there was no telling where further investigation would lead.

By this time both my children were grown and had long since flown the nest. However, having a daughter who was not only beautiful but also wise and clever, I decided to find out if she thought my chosen profession was odd or unusual. Over coffee one day I raised the question. 'What was it like with me working in security when you were young? I mean, did you find it odd?'

The coffee cup didn't even hesitate on its way to her mouth. 'Oh, not bad. When I was in school and you were security manager at that shopping centre, you threw half my friends out each Saturday, and each Monday they'd come and find me and say, "Your mother threw us out again." That took some living with.'

I was astounded. She'd never mentioned this before. Neither she nor my son had ever spoken about my career, or even given the impression that they noticed I didn't work set hours, or sometimes didn't come home for a week or two at a time. From my point of view, I'd always tried to cover my absences with planned activities that meant they were happy and busy, and had no time to miss me. I'd also tried not to think of the effect my untimely death might have on them if I got any part of my job wrong. Of course there were always a few occasions when a heart-stopping situation made me think, 'Oh, this isn't good; now my children will grow up never knowing they had such a wonderful mother,' or 'I hope my life insurance covers this,' but by and large I admit I tried not to take family worries into work with me. It wouldn't have had a positive effect on what I did; quite the reverse.

In general, I think guilt goes hand in hand with the working mother, no matter what her job is. I certainly remember one occasion at Christmas when this came home to me with a bang. I was working as security manager in a Midlands shopping centre, and part of my responsibility was to respond to out-of-hours alarm activations for fire and intruder. My pager accompanied me everywhere (unless I was on holiday), and usually only activated during the early hours of the morning. It was hated by both my children. This particular afternoon I'd taken time off to collect my daughter from primary school. Her teacher, who took great pains to ensure that parents were present before she released her small charges, took me to one side, and with that sort of hushed, confidential whisper that teachers use, said, 'I thought I should just mention something to you, Mrs. Jones. I asked all the children this afternoon what it was that they wanted for Christmas. Your daughter's answer was, 'For Mummy's pager not to go off!' It was a thrust from a double-edged sword. Needless to say I turned my pager off for the whole of Christmas Day: if they needed me that badly they had other ways of contacting me.

I turned back to my daughter, and tried again to get some sort of deep and meaningful conversation going about my past. 'Did you know I was a twin? It didn't develop, so there was really not much left of it when I was born.'

There was a pause, then, 'Oh God, you didn't eat it, did you?'

Now I'm broadminded about most things, but struggled a bit with her asking if I'd turned carnivorous before birth. What sort of mother did she think she had? 'Why would I eat it? It didn't develop properly, that's all. I can't believe you'd think such a thing. That's awful!'

My daughter was unmoved and unbowed, and as usual completely truthful. 'Well, you usually see anything that moves too close to you as a threat, and you turn aggression on and off like a tap, and heaven help the driver who cuts you up ... Don't worry about it. You were the perfect mother: nobody ever bullied me!' She paused for a few moments, her eyes distant. 'Oh yes, and there was the time you went with me to a parents' night. You'd just come back from goodness knows where, and I know you were tired, but you went around most of my teachers looking at them as if they were alien beings. My history teacher went on a heart to heart about my future educational development, and when he stopped you sort of came out of a daze and replied, "Oh, she's always loved geography." So you got the teacher wrong and the subject wrong, and on top of that I hated geography and had given it up a couple of years before. He just kind of sat there looking at you. Then he explained that he was my history teacher, and that the paper you were holding in your hand listed all the teachers and their subjects, and you might like to read it before moving on to the next table. You said, "Yes, I know, I'm reading it," and he said, "Actually, Mrs Jones, you've got the paper upside down." That really impressed him.' Then she smiled. 'But it all worked out very well in the end: the teachers were more sympathetic after that. We came to a sort of unspoken agreement: they didn't bother me too much, and I didn't take you into school again!' My daughter was on a roll. She narrowed her eyes and continued. 'And there was the time you came to watch me do gymnastics. I'd done my routine, and I came to find you to make sure you'd watched. You'd fallen asleep, and I made the foolish mistake of jumping on you to wake you up. You attacked the woman sitting next to you before you actually woke up, and it took me a while to disengage you from her neck. Do you want another coffee?'

OK, I thought, I don't remember half of that, and there's obviously a lot of exaggeration in these stories. So, I reflected, I might once have been aggressive when I was woken suddenly, possibly ruined my daughter's chances of making friends at school, could have affected her educational progression, and might have turned cannibal before I was born. This wasn't good! It certainly wasn't what I was looking for, and definitely wasn't an impressive beginning to my search.

Luckily I have an equally honest and open relationship with my son, who's just as intelligent and truthful as his sister. When we next got together I tried the same question on him. 'Did my working in security affect you in any way? Did you find it odd having a mother in that line of work?'

He smiled. 'Most of my friends were afraid of you, but that made their mothers really nice to me. Anyway, when Gran came to look after us when you were away we got a lot more freedom. She let us go down to the village to get sweets on our own.' I thought of the endless safety lists and the phone calls to my mother before she came to look after the children. Oh, such betrayal! 'And there was the time a friend of mine came to call for me. Apparently you'd just banned him from the shopping centre. When you opened the door you both sort of looked at each other in disbelief.'

'What did I do?' I asked nervously.

'Nothing. You weren't bad at all really. He kind of muttered he'd leave, and you said he was only banned from the centre not the house, so he could come in. That was pretty good for you really. Mind you, he never came around again!'

I looked back on what I had learned. My son had capitalised on his friends' parents' belief that I was some sort of weirdo, and my mother had ignored my highly detailed safety and security plans for my children while she was in charge. This wasn't good. There had to be another way to find my answers, without me losing total faith in myself as a mother before I did so.

Right, one last time. I decided to go as far back to my beginnings as I could remember, because there had to be something lurking there that would provide answers. I dispatched my mind on its final mission.

My father was Australian and grew up with three brothers in a small community in the outback. He had a wonderfully free childhood, learning from an early age to make canoes and sailing rafts, and hiding them in snake-infested swamps so that other children in the area couldn't steal them. When the family moved to the coast he swapped canoes for racing yachts of his own design, usually leaving his prize possession anchored off-shore and swimming between it and the beach. His stories of close encounters with sharks were legendary. When Dad finished school he was determined to go to sea, and joined the Blue Funnel Line as a midshipman. He never looked back. He was a superb sailor who loved the sea, but his career inevitably meant he was away from the family a great deal. When he came home it was a bit like Christmas. He came laden with gifts, and as children we could never do any wrong in his eyes.

My mother was born in the UK. Like my father, she enjoyed a carefree childhood, spending most of her summer holidays on farms, and after school and at weekends playing on the shores of the Mersey, which at that time were clean and golden. Her father was chief engineer of the ship on which Dad sailed to England, and the first person he met when he went on board. When they arrived in England it was Easter, and the midshipmen's hostel that he should have stayed in was shut, so my grandfather took Dad home to stay with the family for a couple of days. Dad was seventeen at the time and mum was eight. I guess fate took over. They were married eleven years later, and the rest is history. Mum was the realist of the family; an extremely intelligent, well-educated and organised person (still is), and was both the disciplinarian and protector of us three children – with my help, of course! Without turning a hair, she could sit down and assist my brothers with horror homework subjects such as Latin, maths, geometry and algebra, and I'm thankful to her for not pressing such evils on me (most of my maths homework came back with comments like, 'Congratulations to your mother'). But if I wasn't a fan of textbooks, I was still an avid reader, and am forever grateful that she introduced me to Jack London and Robert Service. From that moment on I was hooked on Canada, Alaska, the Yukon and wilderness in general. No great surprises there. In short, I believe I was incredibly lucky to have the parents I had. I was undoubtedly spoilt as a child and basically lacked for nothing.

My attitude to life was slightly different from that of my brothers. Their leisure time was mostly spent on running tracks and taking part in long-distance races. I spent quite a lot of my time falling off horses and reading. They were both tall, slim and athletic, and oh how I envied them their long slim legs throughout my childhood! I was tall and slim until the age of thirteen, when I reached five foot two inches, and then just stopped growing.

My mind was finding all sorts of useless information now, and churning it out like ticker-tape.

Aged eleven I was sent to a private school, probably in an effort to instil lady-like behaviour into me. Having grown up with two brothers this wasn't going to be easy. I hated that school. I hated every second of it. I'd hated primary school, so I suppose there was no reason for me to believe that my continuing education would prove any more beneficial. At primary school my teacher had been a man with no apparent humour or knowledge of child psychology, who split the class into two sections: Pin Heads and Egg Heads. Egg Heads were allowed to write in pen, and got shiny, brand new exercise books, without having to write down to the very last line of the very last page. Pin Heads had to write in pencil and use every last line of their exercise books. I'm sure that in his eyes this section of the class was an insult to his professional calling, and was obviously destined to be delinquents or drop-outs, sub -educational as we were. You'll gather that I never made the Egg Head section. Now this had quite an effect on me, because I longed to write in ink, and just loved brand new writing books. Looking back, I don't think it was very encouraging or productive to call a child a Pin Head. Indeed, educationally it probably scarred me for life. Thank you to the education authority that provided children with such a noteworthy teacher.

When I finally managed to progress to secondary school, I still found nothing in the hours I spent there that impressed me, or made me believe I was learning anything that would help me later with a chosen career. And, apart from English literature and English language, I never changed my opinion. I remember my first day at school very well. It felt as if my freedom had been removed, and that I was going to be corralled for the rest of my life in an institution that would force-feed me useless information, whether or not I wanted or needed it. I remember looking around in panic, hoping to see something that might signify hope. That hope came in the form of another pupil, Jan Sandham, whose eyes betrayed the same secret – we didn't belong there. She not only thought as I did then, but later became my closest friend and ally; and still is to this day, over fifty years later!

That is how friendships develop of course. Fear, need, doubt: they all merge, and if you're lucky at the tender age of eleven, you'll find someone who shares those emotions, forging a life-long friendship in combating them. For five years Jan and I plotted how to escape the rigours and demands of education. We developed bus timetables from the top window seats of our fourth-floor classroom overlooking the busy road outside the school – timetables that would have done the local council credit. We held competitions to see whose straw hat floated longest in winter puddles, and escaped the more wicked sides of education such as biology by taking the same 'sick' days, then spent hours on the phone to each other praising our ability to outflank the education system.

My only saving grace throughout these years was my great love of sport. I was extremely competitive. Jan had been born with a gammy leg and this took her out of sport completely, until we discovered that by expressing an interest in games she was allowed to come with us to inter-school competitions as a linesman or umpire. She spent a lot of time standing on the sideline shouting 'That was in' or 'Oh, no, sorry, that was out; our point.' Being a young lady of impeccable character, she was never challenged! I suppose we should apologise now for winning a few netball or tennis matches we weren't entitled to.

At the age of sixteen neither of us knew what we wanted to do, so I went off to the local college to learn to become a secretary, and Jan, having spent quite a while debating it, decided to have her troublesome leg removed so she could achieve more with her life. After this mammoth decision she went to work for the GPO.

I have a lot to thank Pitman for: he gave me shorthand! By the time I left college I could type without having to look at the keyboard, but more importantly, after twelve months of learning a lot of squiggles, dots and dashes, I could take down conversations at 120 words per minute – and very few people could understand what I'd written (including me at times). Years later this gave me the power to write all sorts of things about people, in their presence, without them having any idea what I was saying. I loved that.

After college I had to prove my worth by getting a job in which my newly learned skills could take me to the top. It didn't quite work out that way, but with pencil and pad at the ready I went to work in the Faculty of Engineering Science at the University of Liverpool for a couple of years. Although I admired the pomp and ceremony that went with universities at that time, after a couple of years I felt there should be more to life than senate meetings and flowing robes, so I moved on to the University's veterinary field station, Leahurst. The difference there was that I was surrounded by countryside and animals, which made me extremely happy. I went to work in a research section dealing with chicken diseases (its exact title was the Department of Avian Medicine), and worked for the director of that section, who had a great sense of humour, didn't always expect me to know what the squiggles and dots on my pad of paper said, and gave me the title Personal Assistant. As I knew nothing about avian medicine, I thought this title was a little presumptuous, but as I didn't have to do anything other than arrange meetings, organise files, take shorthand notes and type them up, I found I could live with it – until the weekends anyway.

It was a fun couple of years – not only because of the setting of my job, but because this was the time I first learned about martial arts.

During our last couple of years at school Jan and I discovered the Beach Boys, Jan & Dean and surfing. We stayed with all three of them after we left school and went into our separate so-called chosen careers. At the time Jan had a Mini Clubman, so we spent most weekends around Anglesey's Cable Bay, Hell's Mouth on the Lleyn Peninsula or Tywyn, Merionethshire. Surfing in all three areas was excellent, and when it wasn't there was always skate-boarding. That Jan and I surfed as a team was undeniable, even after she had her leg removed. We'd pile the Clubman with surfboards and a skateboard, and spend the weekends searching for the perfect set of waves. The only difference was that I'd be in the water, and Jan would be on a high, windy headland with the car. Surf always came in sets of four to eight waves, and being high up Jan could work out the best waves as they built up. If she thought the third wave looked the best she flashed the car headlights three times; if she thought the seventh wave looked good the lights flicked on and off seven times. I don't think it ever occurred to either of us that this was an odd thing to do. When there wasn't a surf, or there was heavy weather, we spent hours discussing just about everything under the sun, from plans to live in the Canadian wilderness to UFOs. If we got bored with watching a flat sea we drove to the far end of RAF Valley and watched military aircraft take off and land inches above our heads. We'd found freedom.

My activities in the surf suddenly seemed unbelievably selfish. I'd never questioned it at the time, and neither had Jan. Thinking about it now though, it probably made me a really bad friend. This wasn't a reassuring thought, because having spoken to my children I don't think I made the awards ceremony as a mother. I'd wondered if my oldest acquaintance would say I'd been a selfish friend, so I'd phoned her to check. She asked if I'd been drinking, and that she didn't know what I was talking about. I reminded her that I don't drink, and she'd replied, 'Good! You're just going senile then!' I put this down as a positive comment.

It seemed best to move on and open another box: I'd forgotten most of this stuff! So there I was working at the veterinary field station, and knew that sitting quietly taking notes, typing them, correcting them, correcting them again, and possibly again, then filing the appropriate paper work, was not for me – but what was? Canada still raged inside me, but as I couldn't afford to go there I did the next best thing and bought myself a horse – or, to be truthful, my parents bought it for me. I was still spoilt: not an attractive attribute.

In the end I had three horses (Ben, Blue and Bosun), but luckily not all together. Ben, a gentle grey who turned psychotic at the sound of a tractor (this caused problems because I stabled him at a local farm), took me through a hedge one evening when we met a combine harvester on a narrow lane. Had he tried to jump it I'd have been more impressed. We'd looked at each other thoughtfully as I sat in front of him, muddied, bloodied and bowed, having gone over his head halfway through the hedge. His rolling eyes had beseeched me not to put him through that again, and as I picked bits of leaf, branch and nettle from my bruised body I had verbally beseeched the same thing! He went to a lovely family in the middle of a busy town.

Blue came next. Virtually bomb-proof, he could be ridden anywhere: he loved tractors, enjoyed farm life and would have been ideal if he hadn't hated men, all men, and chased the farmer up the nearest tree in the orchard. I didn't have much history about his previous owners, but I imagine at least one of them had been male and hadn't treated him well. By the time the farmer had spent another couple of hours in a tree, Blue had to go. I sold him to a mother and daughter who had their own land, with not a male in sight.

Much as I loved horses, owning them had got to be too much like hard work. Still, third time lucky, and I went to look at a locally advertised horse called Bosun. As his name began with B it seemed to be fate that he would become my third horse. He turned out to be practically perfect. If he had a fault at all, it was seeing things that weren't there, or dancing sideways, snorting, down a busy main road, holding up miles of cars and furious drivers. On a cold, crisp day one Christmas I was riding him down a busy road not far from home when he saw one of his imaginary scary things. After going stiff-legged sideways for a couple of yards, he suddenly bolted down the road, scattering pedestrians in all directions and forcing oncoming traffic to mount the pavement. A few weeks earlier, the local council had placed a large, heavily decorated Christmas tree on a traffic island at the bottom of the road, and this suddenly loomed in front of us. Bosun never hesitated when we hit, possibly because he never saw the guy ropes that were holding the tree in place. When he caught the first of these with his front legs he must have thought his scary thing had got him. He stumbled, throwing me round his neck, then with a supreme effort he recovered, spotted the second rope, leapt, miscalculated and managed to come down on top of it: there was a loud twanging sound. By this time he'd obviously had enough of scary things, so, secure in the knowledge of the devastation he'd caused, he put his head up and proudly high-stepped off the roundabout, leaving the tree at a jaunty angle for the rest of the festive season. But for all that, he was a great horse.

Wilderness would not be silenced, however, and a couple of years later I knew I would have to still the beast. I resigned from my job and sold Bosun to a lovely family, whose daughter was just progressing from pony to horse. I kept in touch with her for years, and know that she and Bosun had a great time together. Parting with him resulted in a guilt trip that lasted from Manchester Airport to Toronto – but when I stepped off the plane my guilt vanished, and I breathed the wind that I'd been dreaming of for most of my life.

I travelled across Ontario, Manitoba, Saskatchewan and Alberta before returning to the UK, absolutely spellbound by the country I'd visited. I wouldn't have come back, but I ran out of money. From that first visit Canada became my escape, and a place of sanctuary. Later, the vastness of the country became a hideaway when things either got too hot or I needed downtime after a particular contract. It's amazing how three weeks in a cabin surrounded by nothing but lakes, forests and mountains (and certainly nothing that moved on two legs apart from me) refreshed and revitalised. Canada became my obsession, and remains that way today, over forty years later.

So … no great revelations so far, and certainly no answers. It seems that as a child I fell in love with a dream – to live in and travel across Canada. When part of that dream had become a reality I needed another dream, another aim. Working as a secretary, or personal assistant as some of my roles were so wonderfully called, didn't exactly fulfil any life-long yearnings. Once more I sent my weary mind back into memory, where it immediately returned to Leahurst, and I realised that this was my turning point, because this was when I entered the world of martial arts.

# CHAPTER FOUR
# MARTIAL ARTS AND ANSWERS

My initial move into martial arts followed a short television snippet I watched of a Japanese master performing a 'kata' (a set routine of attack and defence moves put together to practise and simulate fighting techniques). It didn't last long, but I was completely mesmerised by the perfect balance, control and power of that man, totally absorbed in movement and application. I don't remember who he was, but from that moment on I was hooked. I set about finding a karate club, which wasn't easy then, but eventually found one in Chester, run by two brothers, Colin and Rod Williams. It took a good couple of weeks to persuade them that as a woman I actually was serious about joining their club and really wasn't interested in flirting with their male students (they didn't have any female members at that time), and that I would take their training sincerely. After initially sending me away with several very poor excuses for not taking me into their male dominated world, Colin finally agreed that if I came to watch for a couple of weeks, he would accept me as a member, and I could actually train.

I was lucky with my choice of club. On the first night I trained, Colin brought with him a Japanese sensei (master) Sadashige Kato, who had just flown over from Japan, having been invited by Colin to stay in his house, live with his family and help train the fifty or so students at his club.

This was the start of my almost fanatical involvement with martial arts, a commitment that enabled me to train with several world-famous Japanese sensei who came over to this country, among them Masters Kanazawa, Enoeda, Kawazoe, Asai and Tomita. It probably saved my sanity while I was working as a secretary: I found that practising roundhouse kicks to the top lock of my filing cabinet in work was an ideal way to improve accuracy and fight boredom. Kicking wasn't easy in heels and a skirt, but it was good training for balance, and although I couldn't know it at the time it was also good training for the career I later moved into – I usually had to wear heels then too! Unfortunately, I had to stop this when the guy I worked for strolled into my office while I was shutting the top drawer with the ball of my foot, and embarrassed both of us!

For years I took part in national and international karate competitions, competing against many like-minded people and watching the UK's budding top martial artists gain fame if not fortune, among them Dennis Martin, Terry O'Neil, Steve Cattle, Andy Sherry, Bob Poynton, Bob Rhodes and Billy Higgins. Female martial artists were never allowed to take part in competition kumite (free sparring) against their male counterparts. There were female kumite competitions, and we could compete in kata against the men, but fighting remained gender to gender. This didn't make much difference to me personally, because there were already two female black belts, Sandy Hopkins and Pauline Fuller, who would have held their own in any kumite competition, male or female. I competed against both of them in kata, and had nothing but respect for them – possibly because I never beat either of them! It was frustrating to have open kumite sessions in your own club, or a club you visited, but were then restricted to same gender competition rules. Still, I enjoyed competitive karate, and trained with as many clubs and with as many different styles as I could. Each had something to offer, and I believed no style was better than another.

Within a year of taking up karate I was training eight times a week – every night and twice on Sundays. I believe the greatest legacy I brought away from this was the advantage that when I found myself in a position of conflict many years later, it never came as a shock if I got hit or kicked. It was just something that happened when two people or more squared up to each other. It gave me a few seconds advantage over my antagonist, because I didn't recoil, thinking, 'My God, he/she just hit me!'

I loved all aspects of martial arts, the history, the training, the spirit and the thrill of pushing physical training to new heights. Even so, I had been totally amazed when in the mid-seventies Sensei Kato took me to one side after training one night and invited me to join his family in Japan and compete in the world karate championships. I hadn't even gained my black belt at that stage. Unfortunately in the end I couldn't make it because of other commitments – actually, I was getting married. The opportunity never came again, and I regretted not being able to participate for the rest of my martial arts life.

When I travelled across Canada, the one thing I missed most was martial arts training. I found quiet, out of the way places in which to practise kata, or various combinations of kicks and punches, but it wasn't the same as formal training. I knew I'd have to find a new dojo (martial arts training hall) as soon as I got back to the UK. But when I arrived home from Canada with little or no money, my first priority was to find a job to replace my depleted finances. I found one as PA to the headmaster of HMS *Conway*, the Merchant Navy cadet training school on Anglesey. However, the one drawback to working and living in those lovely settings was that there were no dojos in the area, so I set one up in Menai Bridge in a small church hall (after many debates with the village elders). This was followed by another in Bangor, then Caernarfon, Holyhead and Llangefni, and others, until I had seven clubs operational. It became so popular that I was able to give up PA work (with an enormous sense of relief, because I really wasn't very good at it) and concentrate on the greatest love of my life. I was also able to continue my own training and development, gaining my third dan a few years later.

I ran the clubs for many years, and Jan, who had now bought a cottage in the Welsh hills just outside Llanberis, joined me to sort out the paperwork and licences. Because she was (and is) a nicer and more patient and efficient person than I, she acted as liaison officer between the clubs and the local authorities who owned the halls we trained in. From the very first club we built up a team of black belts who went on to become instructors in their own right, and trained students at the branches when I was away. We watched hundreds of people come and train, benefiting from a regime that was originally foreign to this country. We also toured North Wales and the North-West giving demonstrations and practical self-defence classes to a rapidly growing band of people all fascinated with this new form of defence.

Out of the blue a ghost raises a memory.

*It's a dank, cold, miserable Sunday afternoon. I'm standing at the doors of the leisure centre in Bangor. Nothing and nobody moves outside. One of my black belts joins me at the doors. 'You know no-one is going to turn up, don't you? They're not as mad as we are. I mean, who leaves the comfort of a warm house to watch a bunch of weirdoes prance around in white cotton pyjamas – 'cause that's what they'll think.' I ignore him. Someone had to come, surely. Richard, Jan and I have spent weeks organising this demonstration. We're gathering funds to help enable a small group of children from Northern Ireland come away from the troubles and enjoy themselves for a week in the beauty of North Wales. We have begged finances from every local organisation, bank, retailer and Government body that we can think of. We have even invited the local mayor to attend as the Guest of Honour, and despite an official letter saying the mayor did not think he would be able to attend, I haven't received an actual 'no he can't', so am still hopeful.*

*I'm just about to turn away from the doors when two wet-looking women appear around the corner of the building and head my way. They shake themselves free of excess water, look around at the photographs of* some of our more successful competitions and competitors that I have put up for effect and say, 'Is this the marital aids demonstration place?'

'Sorry?'

'You know, the marital aids demonstration, it was advertised in the local paper. The one to help the kiddies from Ireland.'

I feel a bit stunned. 'Do you mean the martial arts demonstration?' I ask almost hesitantly.

'Well, we're not sure. Is that like marital aids?'

'Er, no, not exactly. But this demonstration is the one to help the children. You'll enjoy it, I'm sure you will.'

'Right-ho then, we'll have two tickets; we don't want to walk home in this. It might have stopped raining by the time it all finishes. Do you do tea and biscuits?'

As they pay Jan their money I hear one of the black belts stride through the hinged doors into the large hall behind me. 'We've got two', he yells to the demonstration team warming up in there.

But he's wrong: about ten minutes later people begin to arrive in droves. Maybe they all think they're coming to a marital aids demonstration; I don't even know what a marital aids demonstration consists of, and I don't care; we're making money! The hall starts to fill up, and extra chairs have to be found. When the mayor appears my happiness is complete. I don't know what sort of demonstration he's expecting and don't ask. He and his entourage are there and I'm elated.

The afternoon is a huge success. In fact the only hiccup occurs during Richard's and my knife defence demonstration, when my prized Bowie knife slips from Richard's hand after I block his attack too hard, lazily turns circles in the air, and with a satisfying 'thwack' buries itself in the mayor's chair about three inches from his head. OK marital aids demos, beat that!

It was probably inevitable that during the time I ran the clubs I'd be asked to look after someone: a good proportion of bodyguards and doormen had martial arts backgrounds. I did this first in London, full of confidence in my ability to kick or punch my way out of any trouble that might come my way. It only took a couple of hours of my first bodyguard role before I came to earth with a bump and realised I had little or no idea how to look after the person I was with. This was a good learning curve for me, because it brought me face to face with probably the two most important words in close protection, 'planning' and 'preparation'. The survival of my 'principal' was entirely my responsibility, and all arrangements for their safety lay solely with me to identify and organise. This included the threats against them, their travel arrangements, unforeseen changes in travel or venue, medical problems, blood groups, travel routes, alternative routes and detours, local airports and hospitals; the list was endless. Within three months of getting back from London I had found a close protection training course. CQB Services was run by a guy I'd met during my martial arts days, Dennis Martin. Apart from Dennis, his main instructors were Lofty Wiseman and Pete Scholey, both 22 SAS veterans, and Phil Jones – who would become a lifelong friend.

*** 

It was time to stop the memories and reflect. It seemed as if I'd covered an awful lot of ground since trying to find answers as to how I'd moved from secretary to security. Had I found answers to the questions I'd gone looking for? Partially, yes I had. Was it odd for a woman to perform the sort of jobs I moved into in the early 1970s? No, I don't think it was. Unusual, perhaps, but not odd. Women worked there before me: some members of the suffragette movement studied martial arts in order to protect themselves, Emmeline Pankhurst and other suffragette leaders. Many women moved into the field after I did.

And as for the second question, how had I got into the field of security, in particular risk and protection? Well, simple answer, martial arts; they were the physical stepping stone anyway.

But there was a missing link; a more serious side. There had to have been a specific time when I understood the implications of moving into a career that carried with it the acceptance that, in order to successfully carry out my role, I might be called upon to use lethal force. Or, for that matter, that lethal force might be used against me.

34

Perhaps it was the first time I picked up a gun, or perhaps it was when I first looked at any sort of weapon and realised that if I had to, I'd use it; with lethal intent if necessary.

Part of the answer went back to well before my original training. I remembered as a teenager seeing a news story about a family slaughtered by an intruder, who'd forced his way into their house brandishing a knife. I don't remember all the facts of the case, but the intruder made the mother leave the house with him, presumably as a hostage, and get into her car, leaving her children, husband and I believe grandparents in the house. The family had promised that they wouldn't call the police until the mother was safely released. The maniac then told the mother to remain in the car while he went to get something from the house. He went back, and butchered the whole family. I'm certainly not criticising them for failing to overpower the man, or for not trying to take the knife off him; they must have been terrified, hoping that if they did as they were told everything would be all right.

Fear can be a completely debilitating emotion, and until anyone has been faced with a terror that can literally paralyse, they can never say for sure how they'll act. But I remember being horrified by this story, appalled that an entire family (apart from the mother, which somehow made it worse) had died at the hands of some madman, without any attempt at defence being made. I vowed that should I ever face similar circumstances I would not hesitate to defend my family with the use of lethal force if necessary. I think this is probably the first time I seriously considered whether or not I could react against an aggressor like this. At the time I was probably surprised that I believed I could.

English law surrounding self-defence always appears complicated, bordering on obscure. However, sections of the law state that 'a person may use such force as is reasonable in the circumstances', and that 'a person may use reasonable force to defend themselves or another person'. The problem lies in understanding what the word 'reasonable' means. Not easy in the middle of an attack, when you're scared, injured or outnumbered. The problem is you may only have a few seconds to react to your situation; courts, however, can take months to decide if your actions were right or not.

But decisions at the time still have to be made, and, if at all possible, pre-conceived plans put in place. You have to have control back, and at some time you have to mentally draw a line in the conflict that you nominate as a turning point, reversing roles with the assailant so that you retake command of the situation; and all this needs to be achieved in the shortest possible time.

During my career I'd call this my omega line, the last line of defensive tactics before turning them into techniques of resolution. When faced with an aggressor who perceivably has lethal intent, it doesn't make sense to wait to find out whether or not they intend to kill you. There's no place for 'perhaps it won't happen', perhaps they'll let me go', or 'perhaps it'll be all right in the end'. The thought has to be 'perhaps it won't'. I don't know if there is any hope for the victim who hesitates in anticipation that it'll all work out OK, or who worries that the level of force they use to regain control will be judged disproportionate to the attack; I personally don't think there is. And I will always struggle with a law that fails to support the owner or occupier of a home with full legal backing to use lethal force against an intruder, regardless of whether or not that intruder presents a direct or indirect threat. I believe that if an intruder breaks into your home you should have the right to defend that home, and its occupants, with lethal force if necessary. Period.

*** 

Well, I'd gone looking for answers, and to a certain degree I'd found them. I'd definitely opened a lot of boxes without fully knowing what was in them, and I hadn't been too happy with, or proud of, the contents of some of them. But that's what happens when you go soul-searching: you have to accept the good with the bad.

Did the realisation of how far I'd go to protect myself or those in my care make me different from other people? No, I don't think so: I was just more aware than those who'd never considered it. Would I avoid a fight or conflict? Too right I would. I'd go to endless lengths to avoid one. But if there's absolutely no way of avoiding it, the thought has to be, 'If I'm forced into this situation, I'll win.' As that wonderful expression goes, 'Better tried by twelve than carried by six!' I thought about all the women in the armed services and police force who must have made the decision during their career; that protection might mean lethal protection. Did this turn them into some sort of psychotic crackpots? Not at all. Quite the reverse, I think, because once you've taken the decision to meet the threat of lethal force with lethal force you can put it out of your mind. You've crossed that line, and you don't have to think about it again. I'm sure that every woman who ever picked up a firearm as part of her working life, or served in a war zone, will have made her decisions a long time ago.

## CHAPTER FIVE

# CLOSE PROTECTION, HOTELS, GANGSTERS AND GUNMEN

**J**ohn (Lofty) Wiseman trained me how to use a gun with considerable accuracy, even though I originally failed many times to put it back together again with all pieces present! But if I couldn't remember all he taught me about guns, I always remembered his ethos on work, and tried to take it into every contract I undertook. He was probably the most incredible person I ever met. Pete Scholey, one of the funniest men I ever worked and trained with, managed to convey a small part of his vast knowledge of medic field training to me, most of which I still remember today. Dennis Martin, a well-known and respected martial artist and firearms expert who operated CQB (a bodyguard training organisation) spent hours refining my shooting skills, and was way ahead in the development and implementation of security strategies. An extremely professional person, with impressive experience within the field of close protection, he was also internationally well known for his self-protection and weapons training courses. Phil Jones, no relation of mine but a colleague of Dennis and trainer with CQB, became my mentor and close friend, and I count both Phil and his wife Carol among my closest friends today. Phil made the ultimate gesture of allowing me to use his own firearm, a Colt Officer, to replace the Colt 45s I found so cumbersome early in my training. I also had the pleasure of working with Dennis, Pete, Phil and another good friend, Rod Cooper, during the 1986 Miss World competition, when I was Miss Israel's bodyguard. I can't think of a better background of training for anyone operating in the field of security.

After finding my greatest love in martial arts, I found a secondary love in close protection. I was lucky again: to my knowledge I was the first female bodyguard trained by Dennis, as well as the first female bodyguard Lofty trained outside the Services, and the first non-military female bodyguard in the UK. All this without doubt helped me gain clients who needed a female operative.

All good things come to an end, however. For me it was ten years later when, on my way to training one night, I was in a head-on crash when a bus decided to overtake a meat wagon without looking first. I was lucky once more, because despite injuries I walked away from the accident. From the state of my car I must have had a guardian angel looking after me.

The accident proved to be a turning point. Because of my injuries I couldn't train for many months, and my fitness levels dropped considerably; as a result I'd felt unable to continue working in close protection. I was pushing my luck with the length of time I'd worked in that field anyway. So I had to walk away from the two major parts of my life; martial arts and close protection. It was no good crying over it. I was sure there was something else I could do, without leaving the field of security or personal protection completely.

I found it difficult to settle for a while, so I set up a consultancy that looked into risk and crisis, and worked for organisations that required safety and security audits carried out on their places of work. I also carried out training for their high-risk staff who dealt with aggressive and violent clients on a regular basis. This was good fun for a while, and covered the Probation Service, social services, bailiffs, education authorities, drugs advisory organisations and women at work groups.

A particular favourite of mine was a water bailiff training course that I ran for a fortnight.

The Water Board contacted me originally because so many of their staff had experienced problems with poachers, either being beaten up or attacked with a weapon while they were carrying out their duties miles away from anywhere. Radios for that sort of role hadn't even been thought of back then. Injuries ranged from cuts and bruises after minor skirmishes with single poachers to more serious injuries caused by organised poaching gangs, who carried weapons that varied from long and extremely sharp pointed pikes to sticks of dynamite. I attended my very first meeting with their top management team wearing high heels and a tight skirt, believing it would be an office-based introduction. They'd failed to say, and I'd failed to realise, that our introductory discussions would involve a field risk assessment. I'm not sure what I must have looked like trekking five miles around the countryside, over rivers, up and down steep muddy banks, and under barbed wire fences, dressed in a mini-skirt and three inch heels! Still, something must have impressed them because I got the contract.

Consultancy work was good fun, and I enjoyed it for a while, but I knew it wasn't what I wanted to do long term.

Then, somehow or other, I ended up working for a retail management company which managed thirty-two shopping centres across the UK. I started off part-time, not wanting to commit to a permanent role, but became a security manager at one of their Midland shopping centres anyway. Five years later I was part of the company's four-man advisory team (well, three men and me!), putting in place their crisis plans for everything from terrorist threat to infectious diseases, and training teams of security officers working in their individual centres. I got on well with all the lads, but during my time with one of the centres I foolishly accepted a dare from a member of the security team to take part in a charity event of his choice. He didn't specify what sort of event it was, and I didn't ask. I just took up the challenge. The decision could have cost me my life. The ghost is already there.

The plane looks ridiculously small on the tarmac runway. When I fly I prefer Jumbos or 747s: this clearly isn't either of those. I wonder how it's going to accommodate five of us (plus pilot) without one of us falling out the other side. I'm sure they must know what they are doing, and am just thinking of the safety checks I hope someone is carrying out when a voice rings out. 'Sue Jones'. This is followed by the name of my male colleague who has challenged me to take this charity jump. 'You're wanted in the training room, at the double,' the voice continues. For some reason they all speak like this. So, we walk quickly over to the training room, for my part hopeful that when I get there it will be to tell me I won't have to throw myself out of a tin plane about two thousand feet above the ground. But it's not to be. 'You guys trained for this several weeks ago, I believe, and you haven't been able to do the jump because of bad weather, so you need re-training; there's too big a gap between training and jump.' He says it in one long breath, and it definitely isn't what I want to hear. I'd hoped to escape from the old aerodrome without the final jump, but knew that if I left now I wasn't coming back! 'Right, you two, get on those chairs, and we'll run through it again.'

We climb up on the antique furniture and stand wobbling and waiting for instruction. 'OK, I want you to jump off the chairs, legs together, knees bent, then, when you hit the floor, look upwards and say "big, sound and round"! That's to make sure your parachute has deployed. Got it?' Oh, I'd got it all right. I'd got that this instructor was probably completely nuts, and I want more from a refresher course than jumping off a chair. But there is no time for complaint. 'Jump', he screams. I look across at my companion, but he's already on the floor looking upward and repeating the three magical words that hopefully means you'll make it safely down when the big moment arrives. Anyway, what am I looking at him for; he's an ex-Para, he's probably done thousands of these. I jump and get told off for not being quicker. 'When you're called to jump up there,' he points heavenwards, 'you have to jump immediately, no hesitation, no room for error.' I wonder what his head would look like on a pike. There's one more piece of instruction coming. 'Oh, and remember, if your parachute doesn't deploy, you have to pull the front Velcro section of your emergency chute up and outwards, and hit both sides of the chute very hard indeed. Good luck.' And that's it; we're hurrying to get all parachuted up, and all too soon squeezing onto the toy plane.

'You jump first,' one of the instructors points to my companion, before pointing at me, 'and you jump second. Everyone else, you know when you jump. Enjoy!' Insanity must run through the training team. The plane takes off and climbs vertically before levelling off. 'Stand up ready,' someone yells. I line up behind the person responsible for my being here, and as he sits on the lip of the open door I wonder if I could unhook his chute and nudge him off. But there's no time for sabotage, and as his number is called he propels himself into space. I move forward and sit in his vacated space. What did that guy tell me to do if my parachute didn't open, and what happens after you jump off a chair? 'Two, jump'! That's me; I leap. Wind hits me in the face in a sudden and fierce rush of pure energy and force. Wow! This is great. I watch the plane move on, and another person disappears from the doorway, an enormous white billowing parachute floats above him. Oh God, my parachute, my big, sound and round. Where the hell was that? I feel a momentary loss, where was my parachute supposed to be, where was the aerodrome, which direction was the wind now blowing from – I'm supposed to land facing it. I can't even feel it now. I look up. A great big, sound and round parachute floats above my head – that's good. I look down. Fields and a road – that's not good, I should be able to see the landing field. Now I start taking stock, trying to remember what I'm supposed to do to turn, find the landing strip and land into the wind. How long do I have anyway? There are two cords in my hands. I remember something about pulling them in order to change direction, so give one a gentle tug. When my parachute doesn't fall off I become more confident, and pull it harder. It works, and looking down I see the field and runway below me. I'm elated. But the ground is now rushing towards me at quite a speed, and I still have to find the wind! When I land my face seems to hit first, there is a decidedly worrying crack from my neck, but I can now feel the wretched wind blowing: it blows me and my parachute halfway around the aerodrome before someone helps me stop and unharness my chute!

But even all this fun and enjoyment couldn't fill the gap left by martial arts and close protection work. I'd become restless again, so I left shopping centres behind me and restarted my risk and security consultancy, concentrating this time on crisis management and business continuity. I spent three years working for blue chip clients, major retail organisations and educational establishments, while dreaming of a log cabin in Canada cut off from civilisation by ten foot snowdrifts, where I could eventually retire and write.

Then, a couple of years later, completely out of the blue, I was sitting in the office of a lady called Carol who operated her own security company, discussing training and the shortcomings of the rapidly growing security industry, when her phone rang. Call it fate, or whatever you want, but I think that if I'd been sitting on the top of a mountain that day some climber would have sweated up to me, taken a call on his mobile, then asked me the same question that she asked me: 'Do you fancy working in a hotel?' And I know my reply would have been the same: 'God, no. Why on earth would I want to work in a hotel?'

That should have been that, and I should have left Carol's office smiling because someone thought I might like to work in a hotel. But fate often catches you out – and either it or destiny (and I'm a great believer in both) then takes you by the hand and before you know it, everything changes. Next thing I knew I was sitting in front of a man who operated a company building and developing hotels. He was completely passionate about them, already owned one in Ellesmere Port and was building another one in Liverpool. He made the leisure industry sound fantastic ... and hey presto, suddenly I had become the security manager of a building site – soon to be a four-star hotel. As the man had said, 'I know everything there is to know about hotels, but nothing about security.' It sounded like a good arrangement, even though, if I were honest, I still felt a bit claustrophobic about my role being limited to a single building.

Still, I'd thought, how could I go wrong? I loved Liverpool and the North-West, and it was going to be a great hotel. But after accepting the role I got this niggling feeling that I'd turned left at the crossroads when I should have turned right. I remember speaking to the security manager of a four star hotel in Manchester, Mike Williams, who'd worked in the hotel industry for years and later became a good friend. He summed up working in hotels pretty well. 'You'll either love it or hate it. If you love it then enjoy it, trust me you'll never get bored. If you hate it you won't be there long anyway. Either way you'll know within a very short time. Bet you're like me though; bet you get bitten by the hotel bug!'

Five years after that conversation I'd aged considerably, had scars on scars, lost a couple of doormen to shootings and been involved with one too many gangsters. I would probably always walk with a permanent glance over my shoulder and drive with one eye on my rear view mirror. I'd also known I had to get out of Liverpool, and probably out of hotels. My main problem was that it had got up close and personal.

When they started to build the first Liverpool hotel, the construction company employed their own security company to guard the site. Within a few weeks of my starting they'd proved to me that not only were they inefficient and incompetent, but they were also part of a wider network that traded drugs and firearms. This information came to me via one of their own guards, who was probably one of their better and more honest people. He pointed out to me one night (shortly before he disappeared from the site) that I should come back at around 2am the next morning, and ask the question why men in BMWs with blacked-out windows were dropping off or collecting brown paper packages from the building site at that time before dawn. So in the freezing cold the following morning, at around 1.30am, I sat outside the hotel in my car and found he was right. So I asked the question, and when the reply involved the statement that I should mind my own business unless I wanted to find myself floating down the River Mersey, I'd thrown the lot of them off site. I don't like being threatened. This wasn't the best thing to do in Liverpool, of course! I tried a couple of national security companies after that in the hope that they wouldn't have a particular interest in 'local activities', but when I checked out the first company one night and found one of their guys missing and the other one drunk down by the ferry landing stage, they also got the boot. The second company I'd tried had been no better, eventually walking off site because they were being threatened by the first security company. That was Liverpool security companies for you. I'm sure they've changed since.

In a very short time it became clear that what I needed was a local company that understood Liverpool but wouldn't be intimidated by the threats of the original security company, and one that would work with me, not against me. I needed a company that was bigger, nastier and harder than the ones I'd got rid of. Luck must have been on my side, because not much later I was introduced to a guy called Pete Littler, who operated his own locally based security company. I liked Pete, he talked a lot of sense, and I knew I could work with him. I was right too, because when I left the hotel five years later it was still a protected hotel, without drug deals on the doors or in the lounges, without drug barons in the suites and without prostitutes in the bars. This without doubt was mostly down to Pete and a great door team. His selection of a team for the hotel also enabled me to build up a close working relationship with the lads who worked with me: Dave Conway (who became my assistant security manager at a Liverpool four star hotel, then security manager at a Liverpool City centre hotel, with whom I had more laughs and got into more fights than was healthy); Shaun Criscuolo (who later moved to London to work as my assistant security manager at a top London hotel, and then returned to Liverpool to become group security manager for a fast growing hotel chain, eventually taking over as security manager at a Manchester hotel after I left); Julian Kilkenny (who later stood with me on the doors of a Liverpool hotel and looked down the barrel of the same gun, wondering as I did if that would be our last night); Steve McGee (who during a prime minister's visit knelt with me in a deepening pool of blood following a road accident outside the hotel, as we tried to stop the injured person from bleeding to death); Boyd Fullerton (who one night stopped me attacking a foul-mouthed drunk who came out with all sorts of obscenities about what he was going to do to my daughter – which would have ensured the end of my career); and not forgetting

Barry, Bob, Ian, Eric, Eugene, George, Paul and many more. That my career within hotels was successful and didn't result in my early death was doubtless down to the lads I worked with, as well as Pete Littler and two outstanding Merseyside police officers, who probably wouldn't want me to name them, and whose professionalism and diligence without doubt kept me from serious harm or worse.

Liverpool eventually got to me. It was inevitable. I reached a point where I had to break away from the string of threats and violence coming my way. As a close colleague pointed out, 'once it gets personal, you get out'. He was right. There'd been too many funerals, too many sleepless nights; certainly too many times when I left the hotel early in the morning only to be followed by a 4x4 or BMW. Finally I had to ask Shaun, Dave or Boyd to follow me home in the early hours, which I hated.

I was probably still not thinking clearly when I left Liverpool, because I immediately accepted a job in another hotel – possibly not the best decision of my life! But I thought I could draw a line under Liverpool, the misconceptions, the lies and the betrayals, by writing a book about the years I'd spent in the city.

My new role made me security manager at one of London's luxury hotels. I knew I'd never be able to stay in the North-West and write about the problems between 1998 and 2003 without getting shot! While I worked in London I spent many spare hours drafting the story of five years of drugs, shootings, terrorists, prostitutes, paedophiles, arson and blackmail (and that was just one hotel, let alone the others in the group I looked after). I put in a fair amount about disloyalty and betrayal, then added a smattering of the night I watched an Ellesmere Port hotel burn down and the horror when one of the doormen I'd worked with was shot dead one night. Then I decided that nobody would believe it, put the whole thing on the back burner, and spent an even larger proportion of my time mooching around Hyde Park.

Nine months later, despite working with the help of a contract security team run by a very professional guy called Nana Kodjoe, and the endless back-up and support I received from Shaun, I was back in the North-West. London was great for a couple of days sightseeing, but

I now knew every blade of grass in both Hyde Park and Kensington Park, and besides, I really did miss the North-West. By now, sadly, my husband and I both knew our thirty-year marriage was over. It was nobody's fault: we'd just spent too many years living apart, and eventually divorce seemed the only answer. His job had taken him to different parts of the country, as had mine. But we'd both trained together in martial arts and both worked in close protection (although he'd had the good sense to get out of security and move into education), had been good friends before we got married, and remained good friends after we divorced. I was glad of that.

It came as no surprise that soon after my return I heard that a five star hotel in Manchester wanted a security manager! Within the month I had the job. It seemed I was destined to work in hotels whether I wanted to or not! I like to think I planned a lot better after that time, and that I was a lot wiser. Yeah, right. I forgot. I carried on working in hotels for another five years. I'd been bitten by 'the bug'.

# CHAPTER SIX
# MEMORIES

I was often asked which UK city I preferred to work in, Manchester, London or Liverpool. It was difficult to give an answer, because at the end of the day it wasn't where I worked but with whom I worked that was important to me. Crime and crisis were present in all cities, so my line of work in hotels never really altered. That wasn't always a good thing. I remember walking to work one morning feeling tired, cynical and absolutely ready for change. I turned a corner and stopped at the traffic lights to look across the road into the glass-panelled reception of my last hotel. I craned my neck to look upwards to the high-rise floors of what I personally believed was the ugliest building I'd ever seen, let alone worked in. Some loved it; some hated it; few who saw its distinctive outline, which dominated Manchester, were unmoved by it.

I squinted against the drizzle as I gazed upwards. Maybe it was the weather, or maybe rain had got in my eyes and blurred my vision, but as I turned my eyes away from the dizzy heights a hundred different visions flashed through my mind. I missed two sets of lights, and was shouldered out of the way by an irate tourist who was waiting to cross and go into the hotel; I hoped I was duty manager when he wanted something! I knew then I really was ready to come out of hotels. For the first time in over thirty years I also realised I was ready to leave the field of security. I'd done nothing with my drafted book, never quite having the drive to finish it. This would be my ideal opportunity. I knew I probably had material for half a dozen books, and my mind roamed back through the years. I wanted to get everything written down and published, and maybe, just maybe, someone would pick one of them up to read. 'Once upon a time there was a five foot woman who, unlikely though it seemed, worked by protecting good people from bad people – or maybe sometimes it was the other way round.' Unfortunately I knew none of my books would ever end 'and they all lived happily ever after': that only seemed to happen in films. Too many of my stories had tragic endings.

Then out of the blue, as I walked into the hotel to hand in my notice, I started to laugh at the absurdity of it all: the complexities, the waste of time, energy and life. All the memories were back: some good, some bad, a few tragic and some just plain hilarious. A couple of times I knew I'd been lucky to walk away in one piece. Like a drowning person my career began to flash in front of me.

*The Tara Hotel in London, and I'm exhausted after a full day and evening shopping with Miss Israel. The lads will be back with the rest of the Miss World girls soon; I've beaten them back by about thirty minutes. I rarely travel with them as a group, preferring to keep our movements covert and quiet. She's gone back to her room: she's lucky, she's seventeen – she'll be ready to do it all again tomorrow morning. I'm relaxed about being separated from her: I know the whole floor is isolated from the lift system, and that all entries and exits are alarmed and manned. No-one can get in or out without severe or lethal force. So I go to stick a brew on for the rest of the team in our rest-room; the giant teapot keeps us all going. Then there's the high-pitched screech of an intruder alarm. I drop the teapot and turn towards the door, everything happening in slow motion.*

*Someone who has no right to be here has accessed the secured floor, presumably by force. No matter how fast I run her room seems so far away. When I burst into it she's sitting calmly on her bed doing something to her nails, completely oblivious to the fact that the alarm means danger, and could mean death. Her death. To her total shock I dive over the bed and fling her to the floor, pushing her as far under the bed as I can. I turn towards the door, my hand automatically going to my right hip – but no gun. This is England; I can't carry firearms here. But I dive for the door anyway, aware that I have nothing with which to protect this seventeen year old if the alarm means someone's after her. Unbidden, I have a flashback to the 1972 Olympics and the Israeli team massacre. It's gone in a second because I'm looking for a weapon, any weapon, with which to hold that door.*

In the end the intruders turned out to be two reporters from a well-known newspaper. A man and a woman, they had dressed up as housekeeping staff to gain access to the girls. They were both thrown off the floor – literally.

Another ghost, another memory.

*London: the coach journey to the Royal Albert Hall. I'm standing next to Miss Israel as she sits in the coach and we pull away from the hotel. She's wearing her national costume and looks pale and nervous. There's a sudden bang on the side of the coach. It sounds like a gun, and I instinctively pull her into me, covering her head and the top half of her body with mine. It doesn't dawn on me that someone's spent hours doing her hair, make-up and clothing. She's just a very vulnerable target, and I'm totally responsible for keeping her safe. It's only a car backfiring, and we all relax. I try to rearrange her headpiece, but it doesn't look quite the same. I glance up and along the coach, in time to see the guys responsible for Miss Ireland, Miss Lebanon and Miss West Germany all doing the same thing. Miss United States, Halle Berry, is sitting a few seats away. She looks shocked as well. 'It's OK,' I tell them. 'It was just a car.' Miss Israel starts to cry quietly. I ask her if she's OK, and she replies, 'I'm scared.' I tell her I'll be with her every second, and that nothing, absolutely nothing, is going to happen to her. 'What if an Arab boy gets on the stage and ...?' She makes a machine-gun move. I have no answer for her.*

Memories become fast and furious.

*A Midlands shopping centre. I'm security manager, with a team of seven guys, and at least five of them would be delighted if I disappeared one night, never to return. One of them is an ex-Para: the fact that I'm a woman is enough for him to hate my guts. He's fought me, my training and my authority since the first day I joined the team. As far as I'm concerned this is his problem, not mine.*

*The centre's crowded, and I'm making my way down from the third level, where the control room is based, when my call-sign comes over the radio. 'Centre 8, you need to go down to the Index store. Russian Robert's just gone in there, and it looks like he had a gun in his hand.'*

*Russian Robert's actually English, and earned his nickname by wearing a Russian-style woolly hat when he went out. He shouldn't be in the shopping centre at all, because he's been banned. I've heard that several years ago he had an accident, or a nervous breakdown, and now he spends his days aimlessly shuffling through the town centre and the shopping centre. It seems that no-one looks after him: his clothes are dishevelled, unwashed and filthy, and he smells. He loves to talk to young girls, which results in many complaints from the public and from young female students, who twice a day make their way from the college at one end of the shopping centre to the town centre at the other end. Because there's seating around the fountains many of the students gather there, particularly the girls. Once Robert appears he makes a bee-line for these seats, and this results in a lot of screaming. 'Oh, you smell, go away.' The lads make several attempts to push him away. To Robert this is just a game. He doesn't have the ability to realise that the situation will only have one conclusion. It comes one day when one of the girls complains that Robert has tried to 'touch her up'. CCTV footage shows her poking Robert to make him move away, with the result that he pokes her back. This seals his fate, although I have to say I believe the outcome's unfair.*

Robert doesn't have the ability to separate right and wrong. He just knows that a place he used to visit daily has been barred to him. But he doesn't understand barred or banned either, so he keeps coming back, and the security team keeps on escorting him out. It's another game to Robert, but one he finds increasingly frustrating. Then one day he walked in wearing military combat clothes. Goodness knows where he got them from. Around his waist he carried small plastic grenades, a toy radio, a small plastic gun and several rounds of plastic bullets. It was all a game: he'd come to wage war on the security team and the shopping centre.

With this in mind I make my way down to Index, presuming that he's wearing camouflage gear again and carrying his small plastic arsenal. But there's something different about Robert today. He has a lop-sided grin on his face, and an expression that hints at knowledge known only to him. His walk is almost strutting. I greet him as I always do. 'Hello Robert. Now you know you aren't allowed in here, don't you?' I notice the store manager reaching for a can of air freshener, which he liberally sprays around the store. As it's full of people this angers most of his customers, who start choking and waving their hands around to dissipate the smell. Robert doesn't seem to notice.

'I'm at war,' Robert replies. 'I've got a gun!' He speaks as if sharing information with a confidante, and he sneers, 'I'm going to shoot people.'

Something about him makes me nervous. He has one hand concealed inside his combat jacket, as if holding something there.

'A gun, Robert? Go on, show me, I love guns. I have one as well. Show me yours.' Slowly he pulls his hand from his jacket. I see the gleam of metal, the familiar heavy butt of a high calibre weapon that is anything but plastic, and notice that the hammer is cocked. This is no game. Unfortunately, Robert still sees it as one.

'Oh, that's nice,' I say. His body is tense, and his finger has moved to the trigger. The barrel of the gun is pointing at my chest. I force myself to stop looking at the gun, and make eye contact with him. 'Oh, that's a really lovely gun. Could I hold it, just for a minute? It looks exactly like mine.' I'm aware I'm talking drivel, but a voice at the back of my mind repeats, 'Keep eye contact, keep relaxed, keep smiling, keep talking.'

*Robert is so tense that I feel sure he'll pull the trigger. This isn't reality to him, but it certainly is to me. Then, unbelievably, he relaxes and hands me the gun. I point the barrel towards the floor just as a woman shopper yells, 'Oh, he's got a gun!' Panic ensues. Robert immediately wants his gun back, and grabs it with one hand, his other hand going for my throat. We begin what I can only describe as a crazy dance. The pressure on my throat increases as we revolve around the shop floor, with shoppers scrambling to get out of our way. For heaven's sake, I think, one of the security team must be here by now – and, sure enough, I see a uniform and familiar face in front of me. 'The gun, take the gun,' I urge him, finally managing to wrench it from Robert's grasp. My colleague does this, and I push Robert away just as the police arrive. I've always felt sorry for Robert, but the smell close up is overwhelming, so strong that I don't notice he's broken my finger in the scramble.*

*The police take the gun and Robert into the manager's back office, despite the manager's plea not to: he quickly reappears to grab the air freshener. Seconds later I hear the crack of a gun being fired. It appears the police have managed to discharge a loaded weapon in the office.*

And finally, before I manage to get some form of control back.

Liverpool. I'm on my way home from the hotel. It's about 4am. I drive slowly round the roundabout before entering the mile long causeway. It's my last chance to check my rear view mirror before committing myself to the long stretch of road that runs through open countryside for several miles.

*As I start to accelerate onto the tree-lined road, I check the mirror and see Shaun's Land-Rover following me. I hate having to be escorted home like this, but it's a precaution my boss has insisted on since the verbal threats against me became physical and turned violent. It's never good if a bodyguard needs close protection: it goes against the grain! It's been a long night and I'm tired, so I feel extra sorry for Shaun having this duty before he can get home himself.*

*There's a sudden flash of light in my mirror, and I glance up to see if Shaun's trying to signal me. A vehicle is rapidly closing the distance between itself and Shaun, headlights full on, and even before it tries to pass Shaun I know it'll be a white BMW. It was last time. Shaun must have spotted it before I did, because his Land-Rover accelerates rapidly, closing the distance between my car and his, stopping the BMW from pulling in behind me and separating our vehicles. I almost welcome the challenge because it's been a while since the last one. 'Come on then,' I find myself shouting as the vehicle overtakes me and cuts in front of my car, trying to make me stop. I reach into my side pocket and feel the familiar and welcome cold steel of my baton. I know it's illegal to carry one, but then it's illegal to try to force another driver off the road. I'd rather take my chance with the law if it was found on me than face the consequences of not carrying it at all. I've been in that position before. But instead of forcing a stop the BMW suddenly accelerates, and within a few minutes has disappeared from sight. Shaun is on his mobile to me, and we decide to take another route home. It's just another reminder that I've upset some pretty serious people in the city.*

I pulled myself away from the ghosts. They needed to be kept under control; it never helped to have them unleashed and free to cause disorder and turmoil.

After I walked into the hotel I followed a well-trodden path through the staff doors into the back-of-house (staff areas away from the general public, where guests never go!), down the greasy concrete walkway towards my office. It was the route that room service took from the main kitchen to the goods lifts en route to the guest floors. It's always greasy, and there's always an unpleasant smell. No reflection on the chef or the kitchens; it was just a distinctive back-of-house smell. It never ceased to amaze me that whichever hotel I had worked in, all back-of-house areas looked and smelt the same.

I unlocked my office and sat down at my desk, aware that a hundred ghosts had followed me into the small room. I hadn't invited them, but they were there anyway.

*North Wales. It's a cold and sleety winter's night. I look at the faces of the police officers in front of me. The old hall has a corrugated roof, and I can hear the wind banging a loose piece of roofing up and down: I make a mental note that I must get it fixed. We've been doing PR24 baton and truncheon training. This is the fourth time I've taken them for training, and I don't stop to think how they must feel having a woman half their size telling them what to do. My first session fixed that when I disarmed one of their sergeants and put him on his back in the middle of the floor. After that they settled down and accepted me. The session's over, and they call out 'thanks' and 'bye' as they make their way out into the night. All except one of them; and I know what will follow because I know what he fears most about his job. He needs help, and I can't give that to him. All I can do is listen and advise that he seeks medical help from the police force that employs him. We talk, and he breaks down with sobs that shake his whole body. His fear is probably being experienced by a lot of his colleagues. 'I'm not afraid of dying in this job,' he says, as he has said many times before, 'but I fear becoming a vegetable, getting my head beaten to a pulp, or shot and ending up brain dead, when I've got a great wife and a new baby.' I have no answers, and I can only listen. Stress at work isn't recognised yet, so there's no-one to help.*

It had become depressing, but the ghosts hadn't finished with me yet.

*London. I'm working in one of the city's top hotels and we have trouble with two drunken male Russians. I'm told to evict them because of the damage they've caused. No problem. I go to their room to find one unconscious on his bed, snoring loudly (probably just too much alcohol) and the other one staggering around, yelling in a mixture of Russian and very poor English. He demands a translator because he needs to tell me something. I point to his suitcase and tell him he has to pack. He grabs my arm and starts to shout, 'Translator, translator!' I tell him to let go of my arm, but he doesn't, and won't let me get to the door. The two members of staff who were supposed to be standing in the doorway watching my back have disappeared to deal with another demanding guest. Great! I have two options: knock him out, or wait to see how things develop. I wait: I imagine the hotel group has a strong aversion to staff knocking their guests out. I'm not frightened by either man, they're too* drunk, but he has a strong grip and his colleague is beginning to wake up. Despite my confidence in my abilities I'm not stupid, and I know I'm not in a particularly good position. The phone rings, and the shouting male drags me over to it with him. He answers, then yells in Russian and starts an argument I can't follow. Then he pulls me closer to the phone. 'Speak,' he says. 'Speak.' So I take the phone and say, 'Hello.' I'm not a great conversationalist in situations like this. The voice on the other end of the phone is foreign and calm. His English is not particularly good, but at least he can understand me. I ask him if he is staying in the hotel as well, and he pauses and says 'Yes.' I don't believe him, but I tell him to come to the room and speak to his friends, one of whom is now holding me against my will – which is illegal in this country. He gets agitated and asks me to speak to his wife. The very well-spoken lady also sounds Russian, but her English is a lot better than his. She says they'll come to the room, but she sounds nervous – and when she hangs up I doubt that this will happen. I'm right: they don't turn up. I persuade the guy holding me to let me use my mobile phone. He says 'Translator' again, and I lie and say, 'Yes, I'm phoning a translator.' He still has hold of my arm, but seems oblivious of this. He starts kicking his companion into wakefulness, and I know I want to be out of the room before they're both fully conscious.

I dial 999. 'Police.' Neither seems to notice. I manage to have a few words with the operator before my captor becomes frustrated and tries to take my mobile phone off me. 'I'm speaking to the translator,' I shout at him. 'He needs the room number. I'm just giving it to him.' The man tries to snatch my mobile phone again. He has a grip I can't shake off, not without injuring him at any rate – and I don't believe it's come to that yet. I bless our police force, because I know they've got the message, and very shortly afterwards an armed response team arrives. They take away the two men, and I'm left massaging a sore arm. The police say they'll be back to take a statement.

Two months later the Sunday Times runs a front page article about two Russians who came to the UK to kill President Putin. The paper gives details of the hotel, and gives the name of the person the police believe I spoke to on the phone in the room that night – Alexander Litvinenko. I *wouldn't become aware of the significance of this for at least a couple of years.*

I'd had enough of the ghosts now. They'd moved on to other places without my permission, and I didn't want to follow. But a couple of them persist.

*Liverpool. It's late and my mobile rings. As always a call at this time of the night won't be good. It's Dave. He only says a few words, to tell me one of my doormen has been shot. I sit down heavily. I'd seen the lad only a few days ago when he was working on the doors of one of the hotels. He was a great character. His father supplies doormen for me for all the Liverpool hotels, and his brother is head doorman at a well-known nightclub in the centre of Liverpool; I've worked with all of them at one time or another. I ask the usual stupid questions, when, where, how bad, why, in a state of disbelief. This is the third shooting the family has been involved in, and I can only feel shock and horror for them.*

*A couple of days pass, and the young man doesn't pull through. I attend his funeral, travelling in one of the thirty-six black funeral cars that drive slowly through Liverpool and transport us to the church and then the cemetery. It's an unreal day, with police helicopters flying overhead and police cars sandwiching the procession through the city. I assume they're expecting more trouble, more shootings. We get to the cemetery, where two members of the security company he worked for stand in each corner of the grounds. I wonder if they're 'carrying', and if so whether the police will interfere. But in the end the police just hover and take endless photographs, but they don't interrupt the service.*

Time to put the ghosts to bed and get on with some work, but one more has planted a memory. Before I can block it I heard my mobile ringing again in my mind.

*It's Dave. It's always Dave: his bush telegraph in the city is extraordinary and unbeatable. He's telling me of another shooting, another of our doormen injured and in a bad way. I curse every person in Liverpool* who's ever carried a gun. I curse a society that's allowed this to happen. I curse a city that's allowed so-called security companies to believe they own sections of the city and can therefore control those areas, with lethal force if they wish. I know it isn't quite that simple, but shootings are never complicated either. If you pick up a gun you have to be prepared to use it. Such irony; I'd been trained to do that. Did this make me any different? Did I operate with a safety net and a self-righteous belief that said, 'I was trained, it was different for me?' I'd looked after people for a living, and if necessary I'd have shot and killed anyone who tried to stop me protecting them. Was I any different?

The doorman doesn't die, but he's paralysed for life. Another ghost, another reason for leaving Liverpool.

The ghosts were unstoppable now, and they threw in a couple more unwanted memories for good luck.

*The M53 late at night, deserted for once. I glance at my speedometer and it shows a speed in excess of the national speed limit. I don't know why I'm driving so fast; I'm not going to get there in time anyway. Junction 8 looms up, and I hit the roundabout beyond it too fast and nearly turn the car over. I should be looking at the road and concentrating, but instead I'm looking at the sky, and at the ominous red glow. I want to get there before my boss does. This was his first hotel. I want to get there before him to offer any support I can as he watches it burn down.*

*Liverpool again. The operations director (OD) of the hotel chain has just purchased a new shop, a men's retail outlet. It's big, smelly and stripped of all assets, apart from the filth and maggots that are infesting the floor above us and the cellar below. Dave and I have already searched the whole place. The OD arrives with his solicitor and some other suited person. It's not for us to know the business arrangements. We're needed in case the original owners decide they want it back before the paperwork is signed. Dave and I are uneasy about the arrangements: surely this sort of thing should be done in a nice, friendly, safe office somewhere? Then the OD gets a phone call informing him that the previous owners are en route, and that they have their own way of sorting out the paperwork. Dave and I manage to push both him and his solicitor out of a back window as the front door is methodically kicked in. I pick up my mobile phone and put an urgent call through to Pete Littler: we need back up. I look at Dave, and he bends to pick up a table leg. We both watch the front door for signs of weakness, and I hope that Pete has a mobile unit in the local vicinity.*

*London. It's my last day in the hotel. I promised the team months ago that I would hold a training day for them before I leave. Today is the last opportunity to hold it, and I've cancelled all appointments and meetings, but it's inevitable that at some point my phone will ring. When it does, it's the duty manager informing me that there's a disturbance in one of the rooms on a top floor, and someone has reported a woman standing at the window, completely naked, making 'inappropriate' gestures to a group of builders working on the building opposite. Could I go and sort it out. This is novel, and I wonder if the message has been delivered the wrong way round! I stop the training session and ask Shaun to come with me to the room concerned. When we arrive I knock on the door several times, but get no response. We ring the room, but still get no answer. We can hear loud music and someone laughing, but no-one comes to the door. Then there's a loud crash and silence. I'm concerned for the safety of the guest in the room, so I use my keycard to gain entry. Shaun moves back to let me in, and as I step past him I know he'll put his foot in the doorway to stop the door closing: we've worked together too many years not to know what either of us will do. Inside the room a naked woman is trying to lift a small glass table back on its feet. An upturned chair lies next to it. The room is an absolute mess, but nothing looks broken. I announce my presence and ask if she's OK. She continues to try and straighten the table, showing no indication that she's heard me, or that she's annoyed someone has entered her room without her permission. Then my voice penetrates her thoughts, and she looks up at me. She appears delighted that she's been joined by another person, and asks if I'd like a drink. It appears from empty bottles on the floor and table tops that drinking is something she's been doing a lot of. White powder is also present on a* couple of surfaces. I start to explain why I've entered the room, but she isn't interested, and having got the table and chair upright she climbs on both, pressing herself against the window and gesturing towards the building opposite.

I ask her to come away from the window because the glass isn't as strong as it should be (not true) and she's nineteen floors up (true). She happily responds to my suggestion, jumps down from the chair, then begins dancing about the room. It's really not my position to tell guests what or what not to wear in their own rooms, but this is obviously a very disturbed lady, so I ask if she'd like to put some clothes on. Another positive response from her, and she complies by putting on a fur coat. 'Have a drink,' she orders, 'you must have a drink. What's your name? Come and sit here. I'll order more champagne. I'll order room service. It doesn't matter, I can't pay for any of it anyway.' She talks loudly and rapidly, falling over her words, and then, as often happens after excessive alcohol intake, she suddenly becomes emotional and starts to sob. Her story is long, complicated and at times incomprehensible. In her more lucid moments she thanks me for listening and for not calling the police. She keeps asking me not to, and I keep reassuring her that I won't. If we need the police Shaun can call them. What really concerns me is she's displaying emotions and behaviour indicative of a potential suicide victim. Her mood swings rapidly from happiness that I'm with her to hostile language and physical threats. I'm not concerned because Shaun is listening to every word, and if I want him in the room all I have to do is scratch the mike of my radio with the transmit button depressed: it's a covert system of communication we've used many times.

Eventually I manage to get a phone number for her brother, speak to him, and am relieved when he says he can be with us in half an hour. I talk about possibly needing paramedics, but he doesn't want this. I tell the young woman that her brother's coming to pick her up, and would she like to get dressed, but she takes her coat off again and tries to climb back up on the table. I help her down and get her to put her coat back on; it's better than nothing. About this time Shaun informs me that the hotel's new director of operations (DO) is outside the room with him. Being new, he apparently feels he should take charge, believing too much time has been spent with the guest, the situation should be brought to a conclusion, and that the police now need to be called. I'm appalled by this; we're so close to getting her safely home, quietly, without disruption and without upset. But despite relaying this to the DO via Shaun, the police arrive twenty minutes later. As they walk through the door the woman erupts into a fury. She screams at me that I've lied to her, that I've broken my promise. She spits out that I've betrayed her and she'll never forget this. She moves to attack me, but the police intervene. It's no good trying to explain I had nothing to do with summoning the police; she's not capable of understanding. She becomes so aggressive that both police officers have to restrain her: I'm not sure who she hates more, the police or me. Her coat falls off as she fights with them, and the situation escalates to the use of handcuffs. Totally naked, hands cuffed behind her back and screaming hysterically, the woman is frogmarched out of the room, down the corridor, into the lifts, through reception and out into a police van. Well, that worked well, Mr DO: no disruption to the hotel then, and a good, sensible conclusion to the situation. Well done you. Seconds after she has left the room reception calls me to tell me that her brother has arrived, and is on his way up. Their lifts must have passed each other. A short while later the DO comes to find me to thank me for my help! I have nothing to say to him. There are no words left.

Enough.

## CHAPTER SEVEN
# HOOKERS AND HELICOPTERS

**P**eople behave in the strangest ways in hotels. It should all be simple and straightforward but it seldom is. You should be able to pick a hotel you want to stay in, choose a price range that's suitable, select the dates you want to stay, and hey presto, there's the weekend of your dreams, or the most relaxing day's/week's stay your company can provide while you attend a conference or banqueting event.

Every hotel wants to make sure that guests are looked after and treated well: this makes them happy guests. And as everyone knows, a happy guest is a guest who returns, and with luck brings more family members, friends or colleagues with them. It also ensures they make money, all bills are paid and staff retain their jobs.

To ensure that guests always believed staff were permanently happy and overflowing with the joy of servitude, most hotels I worked in displayed signs on the last back-of-house door you walked through before entering the realms of front-of-house and the guests' domain. These would range from 'Smile, you're on stage' – one of the better ones – to 'The answer is YES; now what's the question?' – which all the hotel chains I worked for used! Inevitably hotel groups copied successful sayings and logos, then altered a few words and reused them. The signs were there to ensure that all staff members, or colleagues as we were so quaintly named, remembered that the guest was divine, never wrong, and must be obeyed, cosseted and fussed over, no matter what the problem was.

This worked for practically every department in the hotel, except security. I can think of a hundred occasions when my answer would have been 'No': 'No, you can't dance on the tables,' 'No, you can't help yourself to alcohol from behind the bar,' 'No, you can't set fire to the curtains,' 'No, you can't pick up that member of staff by his throat,' and 'No, you definitely can't leave that in the middle of the floor: use the bathroom like everyone else.' Perhaps in security we had a different view of our guests. Certainly during my time at one of the hotels I worked in we were asked to carry out tasks that were beyond reasonable, and most definitely beyond anything Health and Safety would accept these days.

My mind was already travelling back in time.

*Liverpool. It's a really hot summer's day, and even the Mersey looks lovely. Dave and I drive out of the hotel car park and motor a short distance to Mersey Docks and Harbour Board (MDHB) land. There's not a fantastic relationship between the hotel and this privately operated section of Liverpool dockland. I've had to do some serious crawling after my boss requested that I arrange for him to have a private helicopter set down on a piece of their derelict land. I thought he was joking at first, but he's a businessman first and foremost, and humour often takes a back seat.*

*Dave's unusually quiet. He drives, and I sit in the passenger seat, which doesn't appear to be completely attached to the floor. I'm clutching a carbon dioxide fire extinguisher and a tin of yellow paint. There isn't much room in his car to put them anywhere else.*

*'Why do we have to land a helicopter?' Dave asks, probably for the sixth time. 'And just who thought that if we took a couple of fire extinguishers with us it would be OK?'*

I ignore the question. I'd spoken to someone in the MDHB office about the landing, and he'd added the request about the fire extinguisher at the last moment. I'd been so pleased to get this far that I hadn't questioned him about the efficiency one extinguisher would have on a burning helicopter.

'Look, it can't be that bad,' I finally answer. 'We paint a great big H on the derelict land, the helicopter comes in, we wave something at him so he knows the H is for him, and we have the extinguisher ready just in case he messes up. You know our leader, he's not concerned with the minor details: he just wants the 'copter landed, and the pilot and passenger brought to the hotel.' I take another look around me. 'We've seriously got to clear this car out before we can get anyone else in.'

Dave mutters something about dumping the contents on the landing site until we've taken the pilot and his passenger back to the hotel. He's still far from happy with the plans, and in order to push his point home he makes one more comment. 'Well, if he screws up the landing and ends up in the Mersey, you can go in and get them. I can't swim.'

When we get to the area MDHB have allocated to us, it's clear this isn't going to be an easy job. High metal railings surround the proposed landing site on three sides. The fourth side drops straight into the Mersey.

'Did you bring a brush?' I ask Dave, looking at the rubbish dumped in the small square of land. He just looks at me. It seems an impossible task, but I tell Dave to turn his back, then hoist up my skirt and start to climb the railings, clutching the tin of paint.

Two hours later we have more or less cleared the rubbish to one end of the site, and there's a barely decipherable yellow H painted on the ground, which hopefully will look better from the air than it does from where we're standing. No more than five minutes later we hear the helicopter thumping in the distance, heading straight for us.

Within twenty minutes it's all over. The H has been completely obliterated by debris, blown everywhere by the helicopter's blades: Dave and I will probably cough up dust for at least a week. Both pilot and passenger are safely delivered to the hotel, despite the guest getting his suit snagged on the top railing of the fence. We didn't even have to use the fire extinguisher!

Back from time travelling, I thought of one of the Manchester hotels I'd worked in, remembering what the sales manager had said to a local newspaper with pride and confidence: 'We can provide anything a guest requests, except land a helicopter. Unfortunately, we can't do that.' Well, that was Liverpool for you. A good 'can do' attitude – we could, and we did.

***

It has never ceased to amaze me that you can start thinking about someone you've not seen for ages, and within a short time you're sitting in an airport lounge, or queuing for coffee somewhere, and that person will suddenly appear.

This happened one day when I was sitting in a Manchester hotel waiting for an interview to become its security manager. As I sat in the sterile reception area I thought of Liverpool and some of the problems I'd experienced there, and wondering why I was now considering working in Manchester. A well-dressed man walked out from the back-of-house area, and I recognised him instantly as a security manager I'd had connections with in Liverpool: he'd been security manager at another city centre hotel, not far from the hotels I was responsible for. For some reason my demons prickled my neck as I watched him walk out. He'd obviously been interviewed for the security manager role as well. I wondered what he was doing moving from Liverpool to Manchester.

My mind instantly raced back again.

*Liverpool. I'm in my office at the hotel, and my phone rings. It's the new security manager at a hotel close by; I'll call him MH. He's just taken on the role, and we met a few days ago at a police liaison meeting in Liverpool. He knows I've had trouble with an undesirable security company, and knows about the threats I've had. He tells me he's been looking through the diaries of the previous security manager, someone I believed was linked to the people who'd threatened me, and that he's found a connection with someone both the police and I are interested in.*

*It's valuable information, and I thank him, not knowing that before long we'll end up working closely together on a case of attempted blackmail against a member of my company's management team. When we've finished speaking I pick up the phone again and ring the number of my police protection contact. I need to make sure they know I'm not imagining things, and slowly turning paranoid.*

As always with my ghosts, another memory followed closely on the heels of the first.

*Twelve months have passed. I know I'm in the last few months of my role as group security manager for the Liverpool hotels. I know too much. The original owner has gone, I believe because of a hostile takeover (although he denies it when I question him) by those he brought into the business, who should have owed him their complete loyalty and allegiance. At the very least they owe him for the designer shirts on their backs, their flash cars, expensive suits and, probably more importantly, their acceptance into the city. But loyalty has been replaced by betrayal. He would enjoy the final joke, though: I must remember to tell him sometime. MH has just contacted me again. He claims he has CCTV coverage of a senior manager at the hotel where I'm based, checking into his hotel with a local prostitute, and also has video evidence of their activities inside. It doesn't surprise me. The escort service this girl works for has been trying to get into our hotels for years, something I've always fought. I despise the manager for his weakness, and for believing that a woman, prostitute or not, could even begin to find him attractive. I despise him even more for failing to realise that it's neither his body nor his money she wants, but her company's access into the three leading hotels in the city centre. Later I'll tell him about my meeting with a lady who claims to be the madam of the service (although I know she isn't), and what I believe will shortly be their attempt to use blackmail against him by exchanging tapes for access into our hotels. The man's an idiot, and honestly believes that no-one else knows about his activities. This certainly seals my fate within the company ...*

I stopped watching MH's back as he walked towards the car park. It didn't matter to me how many people had applied for the job: I knew I wanted the role. I loved the hotel the moment I walked into it; I liked the general manager the moment I met him – a true five star professional; and within a few minutes of meeting the HR manager I knew that she and I would work well together. She talked a lot of sense, unusual, in my opinion, for an HR manager! And she was a Scouser: I always worked well with Scousers. After the interview I knew I could provide the hotel with the service it needed. I knew their clientele would be second to none. I also knew I'd get the job. Cocky? No, I don't think I was: I was just confident; and it was probably that which got me the job. A few weeks later I was officially the new security manager of Manchester's leading hotel.

## CHAPTER EIGHT
# CHRISTMAS IN HOTELS

**B**y December I'd been security manager at the hotel for a couple of weeks. Christmas parties had started, bringing with them the inevitable squabbles, domestic disputes and fights, all fuelled by alcohol and the emotive time that is Christmas.

In order to help with the increased numbers of incidents I'd put on extra security staff to help. I'd taken this precaution every Christmas at every hotel I worked in. General managers were never pleased with the additional costs, but overall it was cheaper to put on additional lads than have guests injuring themselves or damaging the hotel because we didn't have enough staff on duty to stop them.

I have no control over the ghosts.

*The early hours, and only about thirty minutes to go before the party finishes. I receive a radio call from one of the contract security guards. He informs me that a domestic dispute is going on outside one of the function rooms on the first floor, and as a woman is involved would I go up there. When I arrive I find a man and woman shouting at each other, surrounded by partygoers who are without doubt making the situation* worse. *The woman claims the man has hit her; I presume he is her husband or partner. She has a large swelling on the left side of her face, and I know the only way I will be able to sort it out will be to separate them. Not easy when they're possibly married. The other option will be to call the police; after all, an alleged assault has taken place. However, I know from past experience that neither the event organisers nor the hotel are going to thank me for disrupting a Christmas party by introducing the police into the equation, with possible arrests being made. I ask the woman if she and her husband/partner had arrived together, and she replies, 'No, my father's downstairs waiting for me in my car with the children.' This isn't good. It's bad enough when a couple start getting physical with each other, but when a parent's around they naturally become protective, and when children are present it becomes an emotional mess. The woman grabs hold of my jacket and pleads with me not to leave her because she's terrified of her husband and fears he'll hit her again once people have dispersed. Then the husband starts screaming at her, and she screams back, so I move between them and try to calm them both down.*

*More of the Christmas party guests start to gather. Obviously feeling the situation between the husband and wife is more entertaining than their own disco, they group in small clumps around us, no idea what's going on but determined not to miss out on the action.*

*With lopsided smiles and glazed expressions they mill aimlessly around, wine glasses spilling their contents down extremely expensive party dresses. I ignore them. Controlling two or three drunken people is difficult enough; trying to control a drunken crowd will be impossible with the resources I have. I reckon that if I can get the woman into the car with her father and children it will be safer for her, and the crowd can get back to the party. She can then be driven quietly home and it will all look better in the morning – particularly when she and her husband have sobered up.*

*My chance comes when the husband turns to talk to a well-meaning colleague, equally as inebriated as he is, who's decided to take on the role of mediator. The well-wisher puts both hands on the husband's shoulders, then realising he has a drink in one hand, turns to put his glass on a tall* glass-topped table next to him. Possibly because of his intoxicated condition, it misses the table and falls, smashing into a thousand pieces on the floor and showering everyone close by with red wine – including me. About twenty seconds too late he stoops to try to rescue his glass, overbalances and knocks the table, which starts to topple towards certain doom. With amazing agility for one so drunk he manages to save it, only to be cannoned into by the husband who also tries to steady the table. Their heads clash, and in the chaos that ensues I take hold of the woman's arm and guide her towards a back stairwell. This route will take me to the ground floor and the sanctuary of the family car. Once we're in the stairwell she tells me she's a diabetic and doesn't feel very well. I ask her if she needs to take anything, and she says, 'No, I just feel funny.' Not the word I'd have used ...

As we move slowly down the stairs I receive another radio call. Apparently the husband has discovered his wife's absence and is heading for the lift, screaming at the top of his voice that he's going to kill someone. I'm sure this is an exaggeration, but to be on the safe side I say, 'Change of plan. Let's go up the stairs instead.' This will give me two options: an emergency stairwell or a goods lift, which we'll have access to but the husband won't. The woman smiles a vacant smile and turns round to follow me. We make it up the stairs and enter one of the bedroom floors further up. 'You OK?' I ask. She nods, but doesn't speak. She's turned very pale – and thirty seconds later is flat out on the floor, unconscious. Her breathing appears normal, but she doesn't respond when I speak to her and shake her, so I resort to pinching her: that has no effect either. Because I know she is a diabetic and has taken a blow to the head, I radio the hotel night managers for an ambulance. I put her in the recovery position and monitor her breathing until the paramedics arrive a surprisingly short time later. Her father is with them.

I hear over my radio that my colleague has evicted the woman's husband for trying to smash the lift doors, and that he's now outside, kicking the hotel's glass front-doors – apparently unaware that his only audience are his two small children, sitting in a car a few feet from him. I wonder what impression his actions will make on their fertile young minds.

*Another twenty minutes later and the woman has gone, taken to hospital for a check up. Her father has driven her children home, and her husband has disappeared in the direction of the city centre. I reflect on the waste of human emotion that Christmas can bring, remember why I don't drink, and hope the family will reunite happily the following day.*

This was to be the first of many such incidents in that hotel, all in the name of Christmas. I'd been dealing with similar events since I first entered the hotel business, and I continued to deal with them until I left my last hotel. Every hotel in every city centre throughout the UK probably went through the same ritual before Christmas and at New Year. I wondered if the word 'merry' was slowly changing its meaning to something that couldn't be achieved without a major intake of alcohol. Ho, ho, ho.

Someone once said that there's nothing more boring than being sober in a room full of drunken people. Well, I'd change that slightly and say simply that there's nothing more boring than being in the presence of a drunk. I think a lot of guests failed to realise that we'd seen it all and heard it all before. Many, many times. They genuinely thought that their excuses for upset, harm and damage were all original and should be believed by us. They were repeated every party night, and I never, ever, understood why people got so drunk that they stopped behaving like responsible human beings. In fairness it was usually harmless, and a steadying hand or quiet word would sort it all out. But every Christmas and New Year there were always a couple of serious incidents which resulted in a visit to a hospital, or an evening in a police cell.

Because of this I used to get the security lads together before each party and repeat the same thing. I said it so often that the lads would end up chanting the last few instructions with me. I can see myself now, surrounded by the team, all suited, all smart, all holding their shoulders sideways so they could squeeze into my small office.

*'Right! Remember, this is their special event. It's their once-a-year do. Most of them will have come straight from work, so they won't have*

eaten anything. They'll want a drink in their hand because it gives them *something* to do with their hands, and the alcohol will give them Dutch *courage. That drink will hit an empty stomach, and be followed by another glass and another drink. Most of them will be nervous: the ladies because they believe that every pair of female eyes in the room is looking at their dress, and criticising it and them; the men because their boss or line manager is standing a few yards from them, and they believe he or she is watching their every move. So to give themselves courage and confidence they'll drink everything in sight, starting with the free glass of champagne on arrival, then beer or lager, followed by wine with the meal and then shorts or, possibly worse, champagne again when they aren't in a fit state to stop themselves paying hotel prices. Our job is to guarantee they all have a great evening. Make sure they don't wreck the hotel, don't throw up all over the function room carpets, don't have sex in the toilets, and, probably most important of all, make sure they don't lose their jobs the following day, because their alcohol-sodden brains won't have any idea what the word diplomacy means, nor have the control to stop taking a swing at their boss after believing for twelve months that they could do the job better than he could.'*

But inevitably parties still ran the same way. Of course, what made them go with an even greater swing would be the activation of the fire alarms halfway through the night. Moving between two hundred and five hundred sober people out of an event during a fire alarm was one thing; moving the same number of people who'd been drinking for a couple of hours was quite another operation – particularly when the rest of the hotel was evacuating too.

I remembered other times, other hotels.

*Liverpool. It's Christmas at the city centre hotel, and a small fire in the kitchen has set off the fire alarms, meaning an evacuation of the entire hotel should be taking place. Everyone in the party is happy and full of intoxicating liquids; the women scantily clad with only alcohol to keep them warm. No-one wants to go anywhere. I unplug the disco, which causes a near riot, and the lads start to push guests out of the function* room. It's such a frustrating evening that when the fire's been extinguished, the fire brigade's left and guests are restored to their party, I sit down and write my own rendition of a favourite Christmas song:

*JINGLE BELLS (security version)*

*Jingle bells, Jingle bells,*
*Sirens all the way,*
*Oh what fun to evacuate*
*And send them on their way!*

*Oh, Jingle bells, Jingle bells,*
*Sirens all the way,*
*Five hundred cross and angry guests*
*Ignoring all we say!*

*Dashing through the smoke*
*With a fireman on my tail,*
*All the people wave and shout*
*But the sirens simply wail!*

*Oh Jingle bells, Jingle bells,*
*Sirens all the way,*
*How I love this time of year*
*And it's still not Christmas Day!*

I put it up in the security room later that morning to try and boost the lads' drooping pre-Christmas spirits.

Christmas parties also introduced what we later called the 'dead hour dozen'. Usually between midnight and 1am, when partying guests weren't drunk enough for us to intervene and others hadn't started to return to the hotel with non-residents, prostitutes and other undesirables, we took a short time out to compile our twelve favourite guest quotes of the night, then put them on the security room noticeboard until the following night. There were some that recurred with amazing regularity:

'Do you know who I am?' (We never did!)

'I pay your wages. Of course you have to do what I tell you.'

'You'll all be out of a job in the morning when the general manager hears about this.'

'Of course you have to let her in, she's my sister.' (This was from guests who were returning to the hotel in the early hours of the morning with women who were blatantly anything but their sisters!)

And in one classic case at a hotel no more than a year old: 'I've been coming here for five years as a regular paying guest. I'm the owner's cousin.'

I'm sure all this was very childish, but it kept us sane – although I came to believe over the years that the words 'sane' and 'Christmas' just didn't go together. For some reason the majority of people we dealt with around that period seemed to lose all sense of reason. But then, of course, I'm a very cynical person, and perhaps I just got worse as the years went on.

Thoughts of Christmas set off another chain of memories. The ghosts still lingered in Liverpool, but another hotel, another Christmas.

*It's bitterly cold, and shortly after midnight the kitchen staff come back to the hotel after their Christmas night out. They all look hilarious in fancy dress. I see the executive chef walk in dressed as a bumble bee, and I see at least one Elvis making his way to the staff changing rooms. Our boss, in his wisdom, has allowed them to change in the hotel before and after their evening out. It's an act of kindness that will be repaid.*

*Just as the last one comes through the front doors the fire alarms go off. The fire alarm panel shows 'Fire, 1st Floor Maids' Room', so I send two of the security lads up there to check it out, and the other two lads down to the function room to start opening the glass fire escape doors, to speed up evacuation. The kitchen staff make their way to reception to see if they can help. Luckily they appear sober, and as we have a minimum night team on duty I ask them to go and help the security lads evacuate the floors, making sure their own safety isn't jeopardised.*

*I get an almost comical view of the backside of the bee as the chef hurries off to help. My radio crackles into life: 'Confirm we have a fire on first floor. Confirm we have a fire.' Although there's a direct signal to the local fire brigade, I pick up the reception phone and dial 999 anyway. No sooner have I spoken to the fire brigade and put the phone down when it rings again, and I automatically pick it up. It's an elderly guest I was speaking to literally no more than an hour before. She and her husband are using the hotel to recuperate after his open heart surgery. She asks if they have to evacuate, as her husband really isn't feeling well. I look at the freezing, sleety rain driving past the glass doors, and tell her they should both evacuate by the nearest exit, but then if possible make their way to me at the reception desk next to the revolving doors. I see the two night managers answering an awful lot of phones from guests asking if they have to evacuate, because it's snowing! I leave them to it because my radio's going again, and it isn't good news.*

*It appears that smoke from the fire, which apparently started in a tumble dryer, is being sucked up the lift shaft in the maids' room, and is slowly entering the hotel's fourth-floor and top-floor corridor. Smoke is also drifting along the first-floor corridor because someone, presumably a member of staff, has stupidly wedged open both the doors to the maids' room and the first-floor guest corridor. With no seal to stop it, the smoke is getting quite dense. The lads tell me they're evacuating the last of the guests from this floor. The phone rings again, and it's the mother of a sick child. She's on the first floor, and must be smelling smoke by now. I'd spoken to her a couple of hours earlier, because she was concerned about her child's health and wanted a doctor. Now she sounds totally distraught, and tells me her child is barely breathing and has gone completely limp. I redirect one of the lads to her room, to give immediate first aid if needed and to guide both parents and child to me in reception if possible. Then I put my second 999 call in, for an ambulance.*

*Once more, as soon as I put the phone down it rings again. Before the fire alarm went off I dealt with an obnoxious female guest, extremely drunk, who was attending the Christmas party in the function suite. She* wanted to take several, uninvited, friends with her, but the organisers refused to let them in. I upheld their decision, but this gave me a popularity rating somewhere around zero. She came to see me several times to cast scorn on my ability to be a duty manager, a security manager and even a human being, and eventually, not being able to get her way, she told me she was going to bed because I'd spoilt her entire evening, not to mention her Christmas. Now she's on the phone, wanting to know what's going on. She asks if we're all idiots, waking people up when they're asleep, although the word 'asleep' came out as 'ashhleep'; she sounds as if she visited her room's mini bar before going to bed. I tell her we have a small fire in the hotel, and that for her safety she should leave by the nearest safe exit. I hear loud banging on her door. Instead of hanging up the phone she drops it, and I hear her making her noisy way to the door, unchaining and then opening it. I hear her say, 'Oh, you people are quite mad. I'm not paying my bill. I'm speaking to the general manager in the morning. You're all insane.' I recognise the chef's voice, and hear him asking her to vacate the hotel as soon as possible. This is followed by the sound of a door slamming, and she's back on the phone again. 'You people are incapable of operating anything. I've got a giant bumble bee outside my door telling me to get out of the hotel. I suppose you think this is funny.'

Actually, I don't, but I have more important things on my mind. I ask her again to leave the hotel, then put the phone down. Within ten minutes she's back on the phone to tell me there's an Elvis at the door being extremely rude to her. He's just called her drunk, and what am I going to do about that? I retort, 'Absolutely nothing, madam, but if you don't leave the hotel soon it's highly possible that you're going to burn to death, and believe me, I won't do anything about that either.' I really have had enough of her.

The sick child comes down with its anxious parents, and the lovely elderly couple sit near me, patiently waiting for the ambulance. Unfortunately both ambulance and fire brigade arrive together. I can't remember if the ambulance hits the barrier to the hotel and blocks the fire engine from getting in, or whether it's the other way around. Still, minutes later the fire is out, the smoke is being sucked out of the hotel by the fire vents, and most guests are enjoying free tea or coffee at an emergency drinks station I've set up. Considering the situation, I reflect that it hasn't gone too badly, and most importantly no-one has been injured. The executive chef, still in his bumble bee outfit, comes over one more time to see if there's anything else he can do to help before taking his team to get changed. I'm just thanking him when I hear a familiar, female voice moving closer.

'I want to speak to whoever's in charge. I'll never stay at this hotel again. They're all crazy. I've had an enormous bumble-bee outside my room. I've been made to leave the hotel in the middle of the night and stand, freezing, in the pouring rain. No-one's told me anything ...' Then she sees me. 'Oh, you, I might have known. I want to see the manager. I won't be paying my bill tomorrow.' Then she sees the chef's back as he makes his way to the changing rooms. 'Oh, the giant insect ... where's he going?'

'To get changed,' I reply, almost knowing what's coming next.

'Oh, I see, and Elvis, where's he?' she asks, mustering every ounce of sarcasm.

I know I shouldn't, but it's been a very, very long night, and I've had enough. 'Elvis, madam? You've just missed him. Elvis has left the building.'

## CHAPTER NINE
# TINSEL AND TARGETS

I suppose Christmas and New Year mean a lot of different things to different people. While I worked in hotels I can honestly say that I never actually saw a happy Christmas party or New Year's Eve party. I'm sure there must have been many people attending these events who woke up in the morning and said, 'Wow, that was a great party.' But they didn't have to clean up the mess they left behind them. I don't mean the Christmas tinsel, used crackers or party poppers; I mean vomit, smashed glasses, ruined carpets and used condoms floating around the toilets, or worse still on the back stairs. Many a waitress or member of the bar staff woke the following morning with a bruise or two, inflicted by an over-enthusiastic partygoer who wanted to get up close and personal, with hugs, jovial slaps or bottom pinches, all in the name of Christmas spirit. But to partygoers this was their once-a-year party night, and they were going to enjoy it no matter what the consequences to personnel or property. The main reason was always the same: alcohol consumption, or perhaps I should say excessive alcohol consumption.

Usually at a Christmas party everyone came from the same company or organisation, so everyone more or less knew everyone else, and trouble between tables was rare. But most hotels would also offer what they called 'mixed party nights' throughout the month of December. This involved selling tables to different companies or organisations, and if numbers were small enough, they'd even sell one table to two or three different groups, none of whom knew each other. Sometimes it worked and everyone got on well together, and sometimes it didn't. After a few drinks someone would make a comment about someone else's wife or husband and because they were all complete strangers the comments would get blown out of context with disastrous results.

However, it's true to say that Christmas events were never boring or dull. We certainly got involved in many extremely interesting ones, and several were just plain scary.

Another night, another memory.

*Liverpool. It's a mixed party night, and there's a table that we know from experience will cause trouble once alcohol has flowed freely. It's a small group of young men, self-assured to the point of arrogance, loud and demanding. This doesn't matter to the hotel because money flows from their pockets, and that's always a plus. But it's only a matter of time before their loud and coarse behaviour upsets some of the quieter tables nearby. The young girls with them are locals, dressed for a night out on the town, and wearing the minutest amount of clothing possible. Together with their male companions, they obviously care little for the other guests present.*

*It doesn't take long for their group to be joined by a couple of youths who obviously haven't bought tickets for the evening, and they are politely asked to leave by the security team. We could be wrong, but we believe the uninvited guests have probably attended to supply what are so wonderfully called recreational drugs. Not a good omen this early. I'm working with the usual security team, including Julian Kilkenny and Steve McGee. About an hour after they've escorted the uninvited youths out of the hotel, Jules radios me to come to the front doors of the hotel. He informs me that one of the men from the table we've been watching regularly leaves the hotel, and goes out into the car park to meet the driver of a BMW with blacked out windows. They talk for a couple of minutes, then he returns to the hotel. Jules and Steve think he's bringing drugs back in with him. I go to my office and bring the CCTV cameras round to try to see what's happening outside, but the cameras don't adequately cover the area he's talking about. I wonder if this is a coincidence, or whether the driver of the BMW is aware of the location of the cameras and the area they cover.*

*I'm interrupted from watching further because my radio jumps into life with a request for security down at the function room where the Christmas party's being held. The lads beat me down there, and when I arrive they're separating two men who are angrily facing up to each other. Both are drunk; both are from the table we've been watching. The security lads sit the two men down, warn them about their behaviour, and because of their many apologies and assurances that it was just a misunderstanding we leave them alone. We know there'll be further trouble, but one skirmish doesn't warrant an eviction – something you learn quickly in hotel security. Always think about the following morning: the general manager will never be happy if guests have been evicted!*

*The rest of the night passes fairly quietly, considering there are about three hundred people getting steadily drunk together, few of whom know each other. Then, shortly before the function's due to finish, my radio springs into life again. It's one of the security lads requesting back-up at the function room. A request like this always gets an immediate and rapid response, and within a few seconds four of us are back in the function room. The trouble is at the same table, the same group of men. This time the table's upside down, and two of them are on the floor, fighting. Most of the other tables are deserted because practically everyone's on the dance floor. We separate them, and I tell Jules and Steve to evict the two who've been fighting. Their companions try to persuade us to let them stay, pleading another misunderstanding, and the stress that one of them is under because of the sudden death of a beloved grandmother with whom he's lived all his life (I personally doubt any of them had a 'beloved' relative anywhere). It's a story we've heard many times before, and years of Christmas parties and drunks have made me immune to sob stories by anyone, let alone someone I consider as little more than a drunken or drugged yob. There's a brief discussion about their sad lives as they're walked out of the room, mainly by the other members of the group, all of whom are so drunk, drugged or a combination of both that they can barely talk. Their loyalty lasts until they get to the function room door, then the girls call them to the dance floor and they obediently stagger back. I notice that one of the men being evicted is the one who went out to the car park. He's spitting venom, screaming at the top of his voice about what he'll do to us, the hotel and anyone associated with the hotel, and yells that he has friends who are going to sort us out. All quite normal, really.*

*Eventually he has to be manhandled out of the hotel after taking a swing at Jules, and trying to up-end chairs on the way to the front doors. Once outside he starts to kick the glass doors, swearing that he'll 'sort us'. This happens practically every weekend, and certainly most function nights, so we take no notice of the threats. We warn him that if he doesn't stop screaming and kicking we'll call the police, so he can explain to them why he wants to cause damage to the hotel. His mate pulls him away, and our attention returns to the function room as the majority of partygoers begin to leave.*

*We clear the room of the last stragglers, and accompany them to the front doors to make sure that they get on the right coaches, in the right taxis, don't fall in the extremely prickly bushes around the hotel or into the Mersey, which is relatively close.*

*Another radio call, and one of the security lads informs me that the BMW is back. It has apparently come in under the barriers, driven slowly round the island in front of the hotel, then left the same way it came in. I go to the front doors and ask the lads if they could identify who was driving, or in the car, but because of the tinted windows they weren't able to see anyone. They haven't been able to catch the registration number either. I ask them to let me know if the car comes back, and return to my office to complete the evening's never-ending paperwork.*

*We have about an hour to go before we can stand down and go home. I walk to the front doors to check all is well with the security lads there. Jules, Steve and another young doorman are standing in heavy black coats, collars up, hands in pockets against the cold, dark morning. We turn as we hear a vehicle approaching slowly to our right, concealed by the corner of the hotel. There's a slight intake of breath from Jules as the vehicle comes slowly into sight; we all recognise the BMW. No-one speaks: we all have a feeling that this isn't going to be a good experience. The car drives past us, very slowly, its windows dark and impregnable. It continues slowly round the island, then the front window descends and the barrel of a gun emerges. There's complete silence. Life is suspended. A hand and an arm follow the barrel of the gun, then the barrel lifts slightly – and I wait for the impact of a bullet. There's no flash, no sound. The vehicle suddenly accelerates, tyres squealing as it heads for the exit barriers. Either the gun's misfired or it wasn't fired at all. We'll never know.*

*An eternity of silence: probably no more than a few seconds.*

*'Was that a gun?' the young doorman asks.*

*'Yes,' Jules, Steve and I reply in unison.*

*'Fuck,' says the youngster.*

*Another pause, and then, as if coming out of a dream, I say, 'I'd better let the police know then.'*

*'Yes, right,' they reply, sounding as spaced as I did. And that was it!*

*We give all details to the police, including the vehicle's registration. But there's little follow up. The car has been reported stolen, and as there are no bodies and no damage done the incident, like so many others, quietly dies a death. I'm just glad we didn't …*

***

That Liverpool had a gun culture in the 1980s and '90s is never disputed. That it still has such a culture is a subject for debate. I'm sure those who hold official status in the city, or are responsible for tourism and leisure, will always refute the fact that too many guns are on the street, and that if you want to obtain one it's not a problem. When I worked in Liverpool guns were indubitably a problem: they could be easily obtained, and too many kids aged around sixteen to eighteen had them.

When 'security' originally gained a toe hold in Liverpool, primarily in the docks then nightclubs, the city was split into sections that came under the control of a few seriously strong-minded and dangerous people. That they were hard is without question. They had nothing to prove in the area of toughness or violence, and had a history of sorting out their differences with fists or baseball bats. Unfortunately, as younger members joined the swelling security companies, and as the drugs culture grew, they felt they needed more than physical prowess in order to gain respect, and the only answer was the gun. It gave them the power they craved; even if they failed to get the respect they wanted. As I write this, the news reports another fatal shooting in Liverpool, so I guess nothing has really changed – no matter what the politicians would like us to think.

So, the Christmas and New Year period carried with it a lot of hard work, a smattering of humour, and just a hint of a threat that a gun would be produced!

It wasn't always doom and gloom, of course. For two or three New Year's Eves the hotel I worked in invited Gerry Marsden, famous for his song 'Ferry Cross The Mersey', to entertain revellers in the main function room. Gerry was a natural entertainer, and of course the highlight of the night was his rendition of 'Ferry'. The last New Year before I left the hotel Gerry was the main entertainer for the night, but interest in New Year's Eve parties was beginning to decline – and when the hotel failed to book enough guests the general manager decided to cancel the event. This must have upset Gerry, because he hired the entire suite himself, brought a small number of friends and family members with him, and spent the night singing 'Ferry Cross the Mersey' to anyone willing to listen. I never want to hear the song again – but you have to admire the man's style!

If there were ever going to be major screw-ups in hotels they happened during the festive season. In my opinion both Christmas and New Year were over-dramatised and over-emotional, so it was always on the cards that something would go wrong, or someone would get upset over a small and insignificant incident. My mind drifted backwards.

*Manchester. It's New Year's Eve and there are crystal-clear plans about how the evening will progress. The previous year we had a successful firework display at midnight, and this went down so well with guests that the general manager has arranged for a similar event again.*

*Setting up the firework display inevitably involves Health and Safety laws and regulations, and the taping off and securing of a section of the paved area to the rear of the hotel. It also involves the blocking of a busy pedestrian pathway over a nearby bridge. Needless to say, this involves a lot more security personnel than the general manager originally hoped for, which costs more – and inevitably leads to several heated discussions between the general manager and me about what constitutes safety, and just how long this safety should be paid for. We finally agree on placing four additional security staff outside, to stop people inadvertently walking into the firework display. Bill and I are going to stay in the function suite to ensure that no-one can accuse anyone of stealing their handbag or wallet whilst everyone is supposed to be watching the fireworks. Such accusations are made every year because in the scrum to watch the display, tables and chairs are inevitably knocked or moved, and after more champagne at midnight, most guests won't even know what colour their handbags and wallets are, let alone where they last left them.*

*Our additional security staff are supplied by a local security company owned by a very experienced and professional guy called Phil Moulton, who knows the hotel well. When they all arrive we run through the safety and security requirements with them, as well as with the DJ for the night and the firework team which has arrived to set up the display. It isn't complicated. At about fifteen minutes to midnight the DJ will announce to partygoers that in about ten minutes they should make their way to the windows overlooking the fireworks, ready for the display which will start five minutes later at midnight. At five to midnight he is to stop the music, announces again that people should make their way to the windows, and at midnight, as the fireworks go off, he is to play 'Auld Lang Syne'. What could be simpler?*

*We have the usual problems with synchronising watches, so eventually I give everyone radios, including the firework team, and say I'll give them all fifteen, ten and five minute warnings before the fireworks go off. The firework team ask me to give them a 'go, go, go' command. No problem. We check radio communication, seal off walkways, discover from the police that they haven't been approached about the display, then find out a few minutes later that they have! We're ready to go: not even Cape Canaveral could be better prepared.*

*The hotel's conference and banqueting manager has already left the hotel, having been on duty since the early hours of the morning, so the event is in the hands of a very capable assistant manager called Alan Fraser. At approximately 11.30pm Alan comes into the function suite to make sure we're all ready. He double-checks arrangements with the DJ, who has all the guests gyrating on the dance floor, then comes back to Bill and me to tell us he thinks the DJ has been drinking. What do we think? We've already reached this conclusion, but there's very little we can do about it. We agree to make sure he doesn't do anything too stupid, and Alan leaves to attend to other matters. A few minutes later the DJ obviously decides that everyone needs more time to get a good view at the windows because at 11.40pm he suddenly announces that everyone should start to make their way to the windows for the firework display at midnight. Five minutes later, for some unknown reason, perhaps a momentary loss of contact with human intelligence, or possibly because he's drunk, the DJ suddenly turns off the music and announces that the firework display is now starting. This causes instant chaos: no-one wants to miss the highlight of the evening, and everyone wants the best view. So all the guests push and shove their way to the windows, only to find an idle group of men two floors below them standing about and looking at their watches. The DJ appears completely unaware that things have gone wrong. The three-deep crowd at the windows begins to chant 'Fireworks, fireworks, fireworks.' I look at my watch, which now shows about five minutes to go. Close enough, and after all the paying customers are* waiting. I radio to the firework team. 'Mix up with the DJ. The crowd's ready now. Set the fireworks off.'

'What did you say?' crackles my radio.

'The fireworks ... we're ready for them to go off.'

'What?' Crackle, crackle, crackle, crackle.

'The fireworks.' I look at my watch; it's midnight. 'The fireworks. Set the bloody fireworks off. Go, go, go!'

At this point the DJ returns to Planet Earth, and realises his mistake. 'Oh no, they're not quite ready yet. We have to wait for midnight! Make your way back to the dance floor. We've got time for one more dance.'

Bill is pushing his way through wobbly guests to get to the DJ, as the hundred or so guests leave the windows and return to the dance floor. I raise my radio. 'Stop! Don't light the fireworks!'

'What?' comes the startled reply, just in time to coincide with the first rocket as it whooshes past the windows.

The DJ looks up vaguely, and enlightenment slowly dawns as the thoroughly confused guests rush back to the windows. The guy isn't a quitter, I'll give him that. 'Happy New Year,' he yells, frantically trying to find the button to play 'Auld Lang Syne.' But he just isn't having a good night ... 'Happy Birthday to you, Happy Birthday to you ...' rings out across the room. The main doors fly open and Alan stands there, silhouetted. He's had a long day. 'I'm going to kill him,' he says, with an expression that looks as if he means it, and he shoots off in the direction of the stage.

I raise my radio to transmit to Bill, who's standing on the stage looking my way. 'Alan's on his way over and death's written all over his face. Let him through. If he maims the DJ at least the idiot won't be back next year.' Bill stands to one side, and we watch without sympathy as Alan and the DJ disappear off the back of the stage.

Another memory comes floating back.

Liverpool again. It's the staff Christmas party. Someone in the company, possibly the director of operations, has decided to hold one big, happy party for all the hotels in the group. Personally, I don't think this is a *good idea, but nobody considers asking my opinion, and suddenly everyone's a security expert. I hope they've considered the effects of internal politics and hotel rivalry, and the consequence this will have on the party once alcohol flows. The event will be held in the city centre, at a well-known nightclub. Great, I think: not only are we going to get together all the staff from all hotels and throw them into the equivalent of a human washing machine, but we're going to put them in a nightclub, and a notorious one at that. Wonderful! I know it'll end in tears – and I'm not wrong.*

*Staff from the city centre hotels are to make their own way to and from the party, but staff from an outlying hotel are to have a coach put on for them to ensure they get safely to and, perhaps more importantly, safely back from the event.*

*I put on a full security contingency, not only because of the large numbers of staff involved, but because there's an extremely good singing act made up of four scantily dressed young ladies who will entertain during the night. I've already watched them perform at one of the hotels, and during that event we had to remove several hopeful, but legless, young men from the stage. There's no stage in the nightclub, just a small roped-off area, so I arrange for us to separate revellers from entertainers by placing enough security staff around the act to keep the ladies safe.*

*The club has its own security door team, who work for Pete Littler. During the evening we're visited by the brother of the young doorman who was tragically shot while driving home one night (the lad had been head doorman there until the shooting). He comes to check that everything's OK, which I appreciate. The evening goes surprisingly well, seeing that we have over five hundred people attending and there are always ongoing petty squabbles between the hotels. Even the song and dance act goes down well, although the security team gets covered by fake snow near the end, when some thoughtful person decides that the act would benefit from a festive fall. When the white glittery stuff descends we all drop our heads and close our mouths, with the exception of Steve McGee, who foolishly looks up at the wrong time and gets the stuff in his eyes and mouth. We make eye contact once he can see, and his expression confirms what we really feel about such events.*

All of a sudden there's only an hour to go. There haven't been many staff evictions either by my team or by the door team, so I'm starting to relax and count down the remaining minutes. Then the head doorman approaches. 'I think you've got trouble at the front of the club. You'd better come and see.'

Not knowing what sort of trouble I, the hotels or the club could have, I follow him to the door. There's silence outside, an unusual calm for Liverpool city centre. At the very least there should be a lot of noise from passing vehicles. Then I see the flashing blue lights. 'What's this all about?' I ask him.

He shrugs his shoulders. 'Don't know. A few minutes ago riot vans and a couple of squad cars arrived outside, and started to seal the road off. Seems someone in the party's seriously upset them. For once it's not us. If I were you I'd speak to that guy over there.' He points towards a group of hefty police officers, one of whom is wearing a flat hat. 'He wouldn't tell us what it was about, but he wanted to know what time the event finished.'

I look at my watch. Just thirty minutes to go before the crowd inside starts to make its way outside. That doesn't seem like a good idea at the moment. 'That lot armed?' I ask, nodding towards the police.

'Yup, certainly are.'

I make my way over to the police officer who appears to be in charge. There are officers standing behind vehicles, and the doorman's correct: the whole of the street is cordoned off to the left and right of the club, effectively cutting off the city centre.

I introduce myself, and ask what the problem is. It seems that the hotel staff who came by coach have caused some sort of problem in the vehicle that brought them over. The coach driver is now refusing to collect them to take them back, and has voiced his concerns to police that when they leave they'll be drunk, aggressive and looking for trouble. Because of this, the police have decided to take pre-emptive action.

I tell the police officer I'm sure this won't happen (knowing all the time that it probably will), and that I believe we have to control the incident inside the club, not outside, because that'll result in chaos and arrests. I tell him that there are over five hundred people in the club, that *they've all been drinking, and that if he lets me have ten minutes I'll try to sort something out.*

*He agrees, so I go back into the club, ask the doormen not to let anyone out, tell my team to back the door team, and definitely not to allow anyone from the coach party out, then go looking for the director of operations.*

*When I find him he's drunk, extremely drunk. This isn't surprising, because everyone's drunk. I get hold of his arm and pull him off the dance floor. This doesn't go down very well: he mutters something unintelligible and tries to get back onto the dance floor again. I get hold of both his arms and shake him. 'Listen, this is serious, very serious. I need you to sober up, very quickly.'*

*He tells me to fuck off, and tries again to return to the dance floor, so I physically stop him. At last some part of his alcohol-sodden brain thinks it strange that his head of security is stopping him from dancing. 'Wossup?' he slobbers. 'Wossmatter?'*

*I speak slowly. 'We've got a couple of dozen police officers outside who've blocked the club off from the rest of the city centre. They're armed, and they don't want any of the coached staff leaving the club. We've got several members of staff and their partners who want to leave now, this very minute, and in approximately ten minutes we're going to have five hundred members of staff and their partners trying to leave together. They won't make it! Is any of this getting through to you?'*

*Five minutes later I'm in deep conversation with a slightly more sober DO. 'Look, the only thing to do is keep the music playing a bit longer; they won't know it's time to finish. I'll get all my lads and the door lads together, and we'll separate the coached staff from the Liverpool staff, inform the police that we'll only send out Liverpool staff, then keep the coach lot in the club until we can organise different transport. We'll tell them their coach has broken down, and it's going to be delayed by half an hour or so. If they think there's a chance of another drink they'll be happy to stay. OK?'*

*The DO obviously thinks it's time he took control of the situation, so he turns round in a circle a couple of times, trying to find someone to issue orders to, fails, looks for anyone who's sober, fails again, then* repeats everything I've just said back to me. Not for the first time I seriously wonder how these people get and keep their jobs.

Eventually we manage it all. The doormen are brilliant and my lads are brilliant, but the general manager from the outlying hotel behaves like a moron. He tries single-handedly to sort the police out, mainly by offering them money to go away, which nearly results in his arrest. In fact, if the DO (who in fairness has now sobered up considerably) hadn't promised that if he didn't shut up and go away he'd be sacked the following morning, I think he'd still be trying to sort the problem out, despite the fact he can hardly walk, let alone speak. When the dust has settled and the last reveller has staggered out of the club, carefully watched by what appears to be a battalion of police officers, all cold, bored and ready to arrest anyone, I ask the officer in charge what happened on the coach. He answers that the staff were drunk before they got on the coach, then picked all the 'No Smoking' signs off the coach windows and proceeded to smoke. Well done, general manager, good control of your staff then! Still, it was hardly an incident that warranted the closure of Liverpool city centre and an armed police response team. I'm not sure if this is down to the reputation of the nightclub, or the reputation of the area in which the outlying hotel was built.

## CHAPTER TEN
# WEDDINGS AND WAILINGS

The most unhappy events held in hotels, following closely behind Christmas and New Year parties, are weddings.

Again, I have to say that I'm sure many happy weddings took place in the hotels where I worked, same as Christmas and New Year's Eve parties. It's just that they were probably held on my day off and I missed them! Otherwise, similar to festive celebrations, there were two stages: pre-alcohol and post-alcohol. Before serious drinking took place at the evening celebration, things usually proceeded normally. The bride's mother was usually in charge. The success of the day always relied on her level of tolerance towards the hotel losing the cake, the flowers, the specially selected napkins, the bridesmaids' dresses, the bride's dress, the balloons, or anything else that was delivered early into the capable hands of the hotel, only to be misplaced a short time later.

My ghosts were ready with a host of memories.

*Liverpool. It all seems to be going without a hitch. The families are lovely, the bride looks gorgeous, the best man hasn't ended up in bed with any of the bridesmaids, no-one has snorted coke, and the mother of the bride*

(MOTB) has one, and only one, simple request. This is that the balloons are to be kept somewhere safe in the hotel after the evening function finishes, because they are going to be taken the following morning to a ruby wedding celebration for one of the sets of grandparents, and the MOTB is extremely anxious that the same balloons be used. A very simple and explicit request, and one that the hotel can certainly accommodate. I think those balloons have more care taken of them than anything, or anyone, else. As the last of the guests are leaving the MOTB comes to see me again, just to make sure one last time that I know exactly what the plans for the balloons' storage and collection are.

And I do, I really do, even though the safe-keeping of balloons is nothing to do with me; it should be handled by the conference and banqueting manager. However, he will be leaving the hotel before me, and I know I have to be back shortly after 8am the following morning, so I can personally hand the balloons over myself. We have a small dry food store off the kitchen which can only be accessed by a master key held by the duty manager, chef and me; it's an ideal place for storing anything that you don't want stolen overnight. As I watch the last of the kitchen staff depart at about 2am I take the balloons and put them in the store room, lock it with my master key, then, just in case I drop dead before the morning, inform the night manager where the balloons are, write in the duty manager book where they are, send an email to the conference and banqueting manager to tell him where the balloons are, then go home, happy and confident that nothing can go wrong.

The following morning I'm back before 8am and go to the store cupboard to check all the balloons are present. They are. So I go to my office and settle down to finish the things I didn't complete the night before. About an hour later there's a knock on my door. It's the head housekeeper – a lovely lady, whose name I'll leave out! She's acting duty manager, and has called to let me know that she's completed a full check of the hotel to ensure all doors are locked, all fire exits are clear, and that I should let her know when I'm going for a coffee.

She's about to leave when a thought strikes her. 'Oh, I've opened the dry food store-room for the chef. He's in, but he's left his keys at home.' I start to rise from my desk, but she hasn't finished yet. 'Oh yes, and I've *toasted those lovely newlyweds from last night.' Her face has a gooey far-away look that people often get when they think of brides and weddings.*

*I really don't want to listen any more, because I know I won't like what I'm going to hear. 'How did you do that?' I ask, a slight tremor in my voice.*

*'Someone left the balloons in the store last night, so I released them outside the hotel. They looked lovely: they drifted all the way out across the Mersey. It's good luck to do that, you know.' No, I didn't know. It was a quaint custom I could have done without!*

Looking back, the incident had its humorous side. I didn't think so at the time, and I have to say the MOTB hardly fell about laughing when I broke the news to her.

But many weddings had little or no humour surrounding them at all. I remember once being warned by a Liverpool taxi driver, who had the unenviable task of ferrying members of one particular wedding party from the church to the hotel, that this was 'going to be a bad one'. He leaned out of his window in a confidential manner, and said, 'Just wait till you see the bride! Wait till you see her dress!' (I never came across a Liverpool taxi driver I didn't like. They were a constant source of information: news travelled around the city faster via them than by any other form of communication.) He wasn't wrong. The front part of the bride's dress had been designed in a cut-away fashion, to display the crotch of her pants, then fell away at the back to trail behind her. It was quite bizarre, left absolutely nothing to the imagination, and should have hinted of things to come. She was hardly a blushing bride: she didn't have to be; we were all blushing for her.

What made the occasion stand out, however, was the fact that the hotel had double-booked two weddings, unusual in a hotel with four star standards. And, despite a four-page letter to the brides' mothers from the sales manager to apologise for the blunder (hoping one of the groups might just pull out), both wedding parties decided to go ahead. In case of trouble on the day I was shown a copy of the letter, and noticed a very cute sentence in it which read: 'We have our own security department who are trained to deal with any security or safety issues.' Yeah, right. Not many people, never mind departments (four of the lads and me!), were trained to deal with brides at bouquet length, armed to the teeth with a formidable array of mothers, mothers -in-law, and brothers who look as if they'd missed several links in the evolutionary chain. But then, of course, the sales department would be safely tucked up in bed when the alcohol started to flow.

And, just how do you write a report to the general manager the following morning, informing him that when the bride came out of the toilets with a line of coke under her nose (in fairness, the colour matching her dress perfectly) she then developed superhuman strength and overturned one of the couches in the corridor because the 'other bride' wanted to use the toilets at the same time. Hmmm … our training really helped that night.

It's probably a good thing that most wedding parties don't really know what goes on in a hotel booked to host the special day of a daughter or son. They don't need to know that receptionists and other front of house staff will have fully assessed them before they even set foot in the function room. The beaming smile that looked so welcoming could be replaced very quickly once the wedding group had turned their backs. I've heard comments ranging from, 'Oh my god, I can't believe she chose those shoes to go with that dress – actually, I can't believe she chose that dress,' to 'Uh uh, look out, meringue approaching reception desk.' I found that every member of reception staff and concierge was an expert on dress design, colour coordination and make-up. I don't know how they did it but they were wasted in hotels; they should have been working for Chanel or Dior. On the other hand, if the reception staff liked you on arrival you could do no wrong for the rest of the day and night.

Thinking of weddings and wedding parties, my ghosts nudge me to remember an extremely sad incident that occurred during an evening function. It was certainly out of the ordinary. At the time it was difficult to believe that so much could go so wrong, or that a supposedly happy event like a wedding could so nearly end in tragedy.

*Liverpool. My outspoken comments to a general manager about his use of prostitutes have ensured that I'm moved away from him, out of the company's flagship hotel, and based in another hotel. The management team really make me laugh. I think I'm supposed to feel like a naughty schoolgirl who told the headmaster he really shouldn't be using prostitutes during school time because it gives the school a bad name – particularly when he has a nice wife and children! I'm still group security manager, but I know that after challenging him for using call-girls, letting him know about my meeting with their company, their hinted blackmail threats against him, and following up with a standards and morals lecture that would have done his grandmother proud, my exit from the company is only a matter of time. I believe the man is a total fool.*

*Shortly after midnight I receive a phone call from the night manager of the hotel I've just been moved from. He informs me there's a situation over there involving two young girls, and would I go down. He knows the situation between the general manager and me, so I know he wouldn't phone unless it was absolutely necessary. Just to make sure I know it's serious, he puts me onto Julian, who's working on the hotel door.*

*Julian informs me that a young girl, whom he thinks is with a wedding party, has contacted reception from her room to say she needs the police. She appears extremely distressed and hasn't made a lot of sense to either the night team or the security team. The police have spoken to her over the phone, and told the night manager she started screaming, 'Get me out of here.' They couldn't make sense of what the problem was, and were therefore reluctant to respond to the call. Because of this Julian and the night manager both went up to the room, knocked on the door to check if everything was OK, and heard someone screaming and shouting. Like the police they couldn't understand what she was shouting about. As she wouldn't open the door the night manager used the corridor phone to speak to her. He told her who he was and asked her to open the door. The response was that she was **not** the night manager, and this sort of crazy conversation carried on for a few minutes. Eventually, fearing for her safety, the two men made the decision to enter the room, but withdrew when they saw she was only* half-dressed. *Not really sure how to handle the situation, the night manager phoned the girl again. Her response was to rattle off a series of apparently random numbers. This caused further concerns, hence the phone call to me.*

*When I arrive at the hotel I'm met by Julian, who tells me he thinks the situation is probably related to a combination of drugs and alcohol. The night manager is trying to speak to the wedding organisers to see if they know who she is. It's now 1.00am, though, and not many of the guests are sober – so he's struggling. Julian confirms that the police don't want to attend because they don't think a crime's been committed, and they're putting the whole thing down to excess alcohol. It's our problem.*

*When I get to the room I find that the night manager has the mother of the bride with him. It appears the young girl is a friend of her niece's. The girl is certainly in an extremely distressed state, showing signs of confusion and paranoia, and makes several attempts to strike herself in an apparent attempt to cause self harm. She's continually saying, 'This is my fault. You don't understand. This is my fault. I love Lisa, but when Lisa comes she's going to beat you up. She'll probably beat me up. Her father will beat her up'! This is interspersed with, 'I love you, Aunty Claire' (to me and to the MOTB, neither of us being called Claire) and continual reference to numbers that no-one understands. She's obviously a very disturbed young lady.*

*The MOTB tells me that the girl's name is Helen, and that she's at a loss to know what to do. I tell her I think Helen is displaying signs of drug abuse, probably coupled with alcohol consumption. I ask her if she'd like me to contact the ambulance service, as I believe Helen will require medical treatment. During this conversation Helen becomes extremely agitated, screaming that she doesn't want an ambulance or paramedics because she is one. She actually says, 'I'm an Aunty Paramedic.' Suddenly everything becomes 'Aunty.' But the MOTB says she'd prefer to wait to see if Helen's condition improves.*

*Then another young girl enters: Lisa, the MOTB's niece. I'm beginning to feel as if I know the whole family! Luckily, Lisa doesn't look as if she's about to beat anyone up, and instead flings herself into Helen's arms and starts crying. They begin to sob that it's 'their fault', and whatever the fault is, it's obviously causing great distress. None of it makes any sense to the MOTB or to me.*

*Suddenly, Lisa announces that she's very tired and doesn't feel well. She's also displaying signs of drugs or alcohol intake, possibly both, but not to the same extent as Helen. Before she gets into bed I manage to get a mobile phone number for Lisa's mother, but despite several calls I can't get an answer.*

*Without warning, Lisa falls back in the bed, appears to lose consciousness, and within seconds vomits violently, while lying on her back. Knowing that this could be a life-threatening position, I place her in the recovery position, clear her mouth and check her airway. She vomits three or four times more. At the same time Helen also slumps back into her bed, and the MOTB shouts out that she's stopped breathing. I shoot over to check her out, and hear Lisa vomit again as I go.*

*I yell to Julian to come into the room. I know he won't have moved far from the bedroom door. He's in the room and helping within seconds. Soon we have both girls in the recovery position and breathing regularly, and while the MOTB monitors Helen I monitor Lisa. Because mobile phone signals are so poor in the room, Julian picks up the room phone to call the ambulance service. I can't believe it when he tells me the phone's not working. In fact, none of the internal or external phones work, and Julian has to wander around the hotel to get a mobile signal.*

*It's only later that the night manager informs me that having hotel phones not working is a normal occurrence. When I ask him why he hasn't told the management team he raises his shoulders, opens his hands in exasperation, and says wearily, 'I have. Several times. The phones, and lots of other things, aren't working properly now. They never take any notice.'*

*Several wedding guests have now entered the room, having heard there's a problem with someone from their party. All of them are drunk, most of them still have drinks in their hands, and all of a sudden they're all medical experts! Julian and I throw them out.*

*Lisa regains consciousness and stops vomiting, and Helen also comes round, but it's obvious her condition is deteriorating. She keeps trying to hit her head, and at one point when I'm trying to stop her she catches my wrist with a sharp instrument. I instantly fear it's a hypodermic, but realise almost immediately that it's a hat pin! I've no idea where she's got this from, and hand it to Julian for safe keeping.*

*About twenty minutes later an ambulance arrives. In the female toilets one of the night cleaners has found three small empty bags with the remains of a white powder in them. It's very possibly not connected to the two girls, but we let the paramedics know, just in case it's relevant. Helen, despite obviously needing medical assistance, is refusing to go to hospital with them. Eventually the paramedics ask if the hotel has its own doctor, and when I confirm that it has, they ask if he can be called. This causes further delay because of the absence of working phones. When we finally contact him, he tells us it'll take him at least an hour to get to the hotel. The ambulance crew are in an awkward situation. Officially they should only designate a certain amount of time to the hotel because the casualty is conscious and refusing to go to hospital, but like all paramedics they're incredibly devoted to their work, and extremely humane in their treatment of casualties. Luckily Helen finally has one of her more lucid moments, and agrees to go to hospital. The MOTB agrees to stay with Lisa. I feel sorry for her. After all, she isn't responsible for the two girls, and it's her daughter's wedding she's missing.*

Years after I'd left the Liverpool hotels, my conversation with the night manager about malfunctioning equipment would come back to haunt me. An article in a local paper reported that a young family staying on the top floor of the hotel had been taken ill, poisoned by carbon monoxide escaping from a boiler in the plant room above their room. According to the article it was down to luck more than anything else that they didn't die. The paper recorded that the accident was due to a faulty boiler, and as it was classed as a 'localised' incident the hotel continued to operate. But I also remembered an occasion when a CCTV engineer received an electric shock when replacing cabling in the main function room. He told me the cabling there had never been finished off, and that he believed the system was dangerous. We got the wiring fixed, but I remembered the electrician who came to sort out the problem commented that the trouble with new hotels was that they opened to a deadline, and many small jobs went on to become major jobs because they weren't dealt with early enough. I remember thinking that if this could happen in a leading hotel, then how many other hotels out there were opened in a hurry, and were unsafe because insufficient time had been given to complete essential works?

Problems with another wedding are already floating in my mind.

*Liverpool. I know we are heading for trouble when an estimated three hundred wedding guests escalate quickly to over four hundred during the evening. It's something any hotel would struggle with, but tonight we have a shortage of staff – not a good thing to happen at a wedding. The bar staff are experiencing an extremely slow flow of beer from the pumps, and there's a lack of air conditioning in the bar, which makes it extremely hot. Wedding guests are quite rightly feeling that they aren't being served fast enough, and while they're standing, tapping their heels waiting to be served, they're getting hot, tired and frustrated. Not a good combination! For some reason the DJ keeps turning his sound system up, and guests are starting to complain it's too loud. The outcome of all this is the inevitable verbal abuse to our staff, and a security presence at the bar.*

*At around midnight I'm called to the bar because some of the guests have decided it would be faster for them to help themselves to alcohol, and have made several attempts to get behind the counter. The security team's fully stretched. More than the average number of non-residents are also attempting to gain entry at the front doors of the hotel, some reporting that they're friends of the wedding party, some just wanting to come in for a drink. Either way they're refused entry, because of the numbers already present in the function room and bar. We have a fire certificate that limits the number of people that specific areas of the hotel can accommodate, and I'm sure we're close to these numbers, if not exceeding them. Apart from anything else, more people will only fuel a situation that is already heated. We also have problems with guests in a couple of rooms on the fourth floor, the occupants of one of these having managed to put a chair through a window that was supposed to be shatterproof. Because of the demands on the small security team, I decide to manage the wedding problems myself, leaving the lads free to deal with incidents elsewhere.*

*Shortly after I arrive at the function bar I'm approached by the bride's father (FOTB). He's obviously drunk, swaying on his feet, and orders, 'Get me a gin and tonic!' Now I don't know one alcoholic drink from another, but even if I did I can't serve him on legal grounds - he's completely intoxicated. Trying to be helpful, I apologise that I can't serve him because I don't work in the bar, but that I'll find someone who can help him. He looks at me as if I'm mad, then says, 'Do you know who I am? I've spent a fucking fortune here tonight. Get me a gin and tonic.'*

*I'm always amused when a guest asks if I know who they are. It's probably the most frequently asked question when a guest doesn't get what he or she wants, is inebriated, or just feels the need to prove who's really in charge! It always reminds me of the story of the airport worker who was dealing with an aggressive and pompous passenger who asked the same question. Her way of dealing with the question was to use the tannoy system to summon a doctor, telling the passenger that if he didn't know who he was he obviously needed medical assistance, and certainly wasn't fit enough to fly!*

*Not getting a gin and tonic has obviously upset the FOTB very much, because when I turn to try to find someone to serve him he grabs me round the neck and starts to pull tight. Violent physical attacks from wedding guests are really quite rare, so his action throws me a bit. But when he continues to exert pressure on my neck I take considerable exception to it, and bring my elbow back with as much force as I can. The result is instantaneous, and I walk away, to let him make his own way off the floor. I expect a major escalation of the situation once he gets back on his feet, but the incident seems to calm him down. I'm not always so lucky.*

*Another problem this evening is because the doors to the function room open close to the hotel lounge. At 11pm this lounge becomes a residents only area, governed by licensing laws. Of course, you can reason with as many people as you like when they're sober, but try to reason with four hundred or more extremely drunk people at 2am, when they all* want more to drink, and you've got a problem. Once the function finishes they'll all want to make their way to the residents' bar for more, whether they're residents or not. This will cause further problems, because some of those guests who are residents will obviously want to take a couple of friends to the bar with them (this is particularly the case with weddings). The problem for the security team is always how many to let in. Any? None? Residents can buy drinks for non-residents at this time of night, but once you let a couple in all of a sudden all four hundred guests are family or friends, and that isn't acceptable to the licensing officers if they come visiting (which they often do). Neither is it acceptable to the residents who are already in the lounge enjoying a quiet drink – which is understandable. No-one wants four hundred drunks invading their quiet evening!

I've already roped off the residents' lounge and put two security lads on to control it. Unless non-residents are known to us as family members, we aren't going to allow any more people through into the cordoned area. Whichever way we play it, the following day the general manager will receive calls of complaint, either because we've ruined the event for someone because we didn't allow his great-aunt or uncle into the residents' bar, or from residents who've had their evening spoiled by an influx of drunken and noisy non-residents. It's a no-win situation. What always annoys me is the complete lack of support we will receive from the general manager, who in the past has written letters apologising that the security team caused trouble! He used to tell me to write letters of apology, but I refused to do so. I understand that guest satisfaction is priority, but a letter that says 'I'm sorry that you "felt" the security team …' instead of 'I apologise for the security team' is better! Personally I don't mind, but I mind for the lads, who work extremely hard to get it right. Having someone apologise for your behaviour after you've put everything into de-escalating or defusing a volatile or aggressive situation isn't a good way to build respect and loyalty (which is probably why that particular general manager didn't get any!). It certainly doesn't go down well the following day after you've spent the night being kicked, spat at, thumped or near-strangled while trying to maintain peace and calm. What general managers crave are no complaints, from anyone, and *that's never going to happen. We even tried pre-arranged written agreements with the organisers of private functions confirming that after the party residents would be allowed to take two guests, and only two guests, back to the bar. In the cool light of day this was happily agreed to. Needless to say this worked well until everyone started drinking, then agreements were forgotten, and the result inevitably was arguments, threats and abuse in the early hours of the morning.*

*So, at this particular wedding party, which finishes at 2am, we go through the usual arguments about who gets access to the residents' bar and who doesn't. We eventually allow four non-residents in: two of them are the parents of the best man, and the other two are an extremely nice elderly couple who only want a cup of tea. Unfortunately, already in the bar is a regular resident who's been woken up by the wedding disco music: the hotel has allocated him a room directly over the function room (I'll say no more). He's annoyed by the fact that the disco has woken him, but has been extremely pleasant about the whole situation. Unfortunately the FOTB bumps into him, and makes the comment that he thinks the hotel is 'fucking shit'. Our resident, I'll call him Mr Hughes, takes exception to this, and points out that he thinks it's one of the best he's ever experienced. The FOTB repeats that the hotel is 'fucking shit because the bar's closed' (which it isn't!). Mr Hughes again replies that the hotel is one of the best he's stayed in. The FOTB tells Mr Hughes how much he's spent on his daughter's wedding, his suit, his tie and his shoes. He says that he's stayed in hotels all over the world (which I seriously doubt!), and that this is by far the worst. Mr Hughes replies that he's stayed in hotels all over the world (which he has!), and that he doesn't think the chap knows what he's talking about. By now blows are being threatened by both sides, so one of the security lads, Steve McGee, steps between them and calms the situation down.*

*About an hour later both men use the toilets at the same time, and the whole situation flares up again. This time the FOTB threatens to knife Mr Hughes, a threat that's extended to all security staff when they turn up. Things have now gone far enough in my view, even for a wedding. So I point out to the FOTB just how devastated his daughter will be if the police arrest him, and he spends the rest of her special day behind bars.*

*To my utmost surprise he bursts into tears, says how beautiful his daughter looks, and takes himself off to bed. I learn a valuable lesson: when dealing with an aggressive FOTB, talk about their daughters – they're reduced to mush in minutes.*

*But the evening hasn't finished with me yet. A short time later I'm in reception when a bridesmaid comes across to say the bride's upset and can I go and apologise to her. Confused, I go to the bar and ask the bride what's upset her. She doesn't make much sense (oh when will brides and grooms learn to go to bed after their reception and not drink more champagne?), but the bridesmaid pulls me to one side. 'She's the most nervous person in the world. Everything upsets her. Please can you just apologise to her.' Now so long as it's me doing the apologising, and as long as I'm only saying sorry for me, I'm happy to apologise to anyone for anything if it makes them happy. I might not mean it but I'm happy to do it, particularly when I know they won't remember anything about it the following morning. So I ask the bridesmaid again what I'm apologising for, and discover it's for not allowing a friend of the bride into the residents' bar. So I turn back to the bride, and duly say I'm sorry she's upset on her wedding day, and apologise for not letting her friend into the bar. At this, the bride bursts into louder sobs and says she isn't upset about that, she's upset about the 'other incident'. Not having a clue what she's referring to, I foolishly make a guess. 'You mean the incident in the toilets?' The bride's now sobbing loudly. She says she doesn't know what I'm talking about; what incident in the toilet, and was it anything to do with a member of her party? I'm a beaten woman; we really aren't getting anywhere. In the end she just asks for another drink – a brandy! As the bar's now closed I say I'll arrange for it to be sent up to her room. Room service later inform me that they duly took the brandy up to the suite only to find it empty. They return several times, but there was never anyone there. I've no idea where the bride and groom slept that night, but it certainly wasn't in the bridal suite!*

So much for weddings. None, though, can ever compete with a wedding held at a Liverpool city centre hotel. At the end of that evening all members of the party filed quietly out of the function suite, and shook hands with each member of the security team before finally leaving. Once outside they split into two groups, produced bladed weapons from goodness knows where, and proceeded to fight each other. There were so many of them that the whole of the city centre was sealed off by the police, who eventually sent in riot squads to move them on and to make arrests. Obviously someone said something to upset someone. That's weddings for you!

Birthday parties weren't always much better. A Greek birthday celebration in a London hotel ground to a halt when members of the party kept fighting each other. It was unusual for this to happen at a Greek event, so something must have upset them that we weren't privy to. For some reason best known to himself, the conference and banqueting manager decided the party must be stopped, and also decided that security should handle it. Shaun and Nana were both on duty, so the three of us went up to the function room to see why a quiet word in someone's ear wouldn't work better than a total cessation of the event. When we entered the room small scuffles were still going on, largely ignored by the rest of the group, whose numbers must have been close to five hundred. We were about to go over to the troublesome groups when the C&B manager rushed up and demanded I switch off the disco, make an announcement to the party that they would all be asked to leave if they didn't stop fighting, and then if that didn't do the trick I should clear the room of every guest! I'd never come across this attitude in a manager before, certainly not in a manager who worked in a hotel, and absolutely, definitely not in a C&B manager. To my annoyance he then went over to the light switches, and turned all the lights up (always an indication that an event is over). Not satisfied with this, he marched over to the disco and told the DJ to stop playing. By now all faces were looking in his direction. The disco guy refused to stop, and told him to lower the lights again, then half a dozen very angry Greeks approached him with hands waving, gesticulating wildly, and obviously not happy that their event seemed doomed to end. For a few seconds there was complete chaos. If I could have dragged the manager out of the room I would have done so, but it was too late. The guy frantically summoned me over; a bit rich, really,

106

seeing he'd created most of the problems himself. In the end, and because no one could actually hear anything over the disco, I climbed up on the stage and unplugged it myself. After all, what was one more outraged person among so many? This caused hundreds of voices to be raised in anger, and an immediate surge of people towards the stage. I grabbed the microphone from the disco and, praying it was connected, asked the now furious crowd to give me their attention. They obviously wanted to give me more than their attention, but despite their anger they slowed their forward movement towards the stage. Shaun and Nana had positioned themselves below me in front of the stage, and before I started to speak they turned their heads to look up at me, their eyes carrying the same message: 'Get this wrong and we'll all probably die!' Twenty minutes later the disco was restarted: the warring groups had promised not to fight any more, the organiser of the event thought it had all been a very funny interlude (thank goodness for people with a sense of humour), and the C&B manager had handed over to his second in command, then gone home. He really didn't have a future career in hotels!

## CHAPTER ELEVEN
# THE LAW AND BRITISH JUSTICE

I don't know how many times I've stood in a court of law in order to give evidence, but it's quite a few. When I worked as a security manager in shopping centres across the UK, we were often involved in cases of theft or assault. Theft usually occurred in the shops, and assaults usually occurred when members of the security team went to investigate the theft!

It didn't take me long to realise that in a court room there appears to be little difference between the accused or the defendant; and witnesses, in my opinion, were people used by both counsels to entertain one another as they shouted at them, bullied them and generally insulted them. On more than one occasion I've been addressed with, 'I put it to you, Mrs Jones, that you're not exactly telling the truth.' This used to incense me. My reply should have been, 'And you, Sir, are an arrogant troglodytic bipedal.' Luckily I usually managed to stay silent, or the accused wouldn't have been the only one facing a prison sentence. I once replied in a magistrates' court to the accusation that I wasn't exactly telling the truth by countering with, 'I'd point out to you, Sir, that I've just sworn on the Bible to tell the truth, the whole truth and nothing but the truth, and much as I would take my chances in this court of law with an untruth, I wouldn't want to try the same thing with God when and if I ever meet him.' This resulted in uproar in court and a reprimand from the judge.

I never actually came away from a court believing that truth had been told by anyone (except me of course), and that the outcome was a just and rightful result. The only things that seemed to matter were the games played out between the defence and prosecuting counsels. The rest of us were mere pawns on a chessboard. I'm not even sure that evidence itself was of much importance. It was how you played with and presented the evidence and the witnesses that counted, and usually the brighter and quicker member of counsel won. It always seemed that deference was given to a defence counsel who was either aggressive or a QC (Queen's Counsel), particularly if the prosecuting counsel was a young and spotty youth representing the Crown Prosecution Service (CPS), for which I have little but contempt because of – in my opinion – their complete incompetence and disorganisation. Perhaps I'm biased and too judgemental after losing too many cases.

Once again ghosts bring memories back.

*The Midlands. It's just another day in the shopping centre. A member of the security team has given chase after a female shoplifter grabs a handbag from an inattentive shopper and runs out of the centre. The unlucky security officer catches her just outside the doors and, being male with a female offender, holds her lightly by her arm until back-up arrives (female shoplifters always seem more prone to fight and to carry a weapon than their male counterparts, in my experience). Slightly out of breath, and because he's holding onto her, thus restricting her liberty, he runs through the legal formalities of an arrest. He informs her who he is, who he represents, and that he's arresting her for the theft of a handbag; then he cautions her afterwards as the law demands. Unfortunately, the young thief has rifled through the handbag as she ran from the centre, dropping it at the exit doors and leaving only with a purse full of money. She will later be released from court on a technicality because she had not in fact stolen the handbag, merely the purse.*

Theft is defined as 'The dishonest appropriation of property belonging to another with the intention of permanently depriving', and all points have to be proved. No doubt the magistrate in this case thought that as the thief hadn't permanently deprived the shopper of her handbag (merely her purse and money), there was no offence to answer. We learned quickly after that.

I also remember a frustrating court case after being involved in a fight with a freelance photographer in front of Kylie Minogue's car one night when she was being driven away from a hotel in Manchester. It emphasised not only the complete contempt I had for the CPS but also for the paparazzi who haunt the rich and famous.

Kylie (without doubt one of the nicest celebrities I've ever met) had been staying in the hotel for a couple of days, and both Bill and I had ensured her safe arrival and departure from the back of the hotel via its loading bay. We'd also become friendly with her long-time driver Alan Dallo, an incredibly nice guy who took her safety and security very seriously. Kylie was travelling with a female close protection operative, who was also an extremely pleasant person; all in all it was a very enjoyable week. However, one of the problems Alan had when driving to and from the hotel were the many photographers and autograph hunters who inevitably gathered to catch sight of the star, or to obtain photographs or autographs. This procedure was part of my daily life when we had VIPs or famous celebrities staying. Because of the hotel's reputation, this was more or less a daily occurrence.

Most autograph hunters and photographers were no more than annoying. I understood that they had a job to do if they were from a national or international paper or magazine. I also understood that fans of the celebrities were there to gaze on their idols, get as close as they could to them, and if at all possible obtain a photograph and autograph at the same time. In fairness most celebrities owed their fame and fortune to these people, and most celebs understood this, taking time to give the fans what they wanted.

However, there's a fine line between allowing fans to get close to their idols, obtain pictures and signatures, and leave (both parties happy with the outcome), and allowing fans to recklessly push and elbow their way forward, not caring whether anyone (including the celebrity) gets injured in the scrum. One threat, of course, was the fan whose reason for being there was both sinister and dangerous. The fate of people such as John Lennon was a sad testament to them. As in close protection, part of my role was to ensure there was sufficient safe space or a controlled area where fan and celebrity could meet without threat or injury on either side.

Alan had been concerned that during night-time departures from the hotel, when he drove up the ramp from the loading bay to get to the main road, flashing cameras used by photographers standing at the top of the ramp could blind him. Because of this, Bill would see Kylie and her party safely into her vehicle, then lift the loading bay shutter to allow the car out, while I cleared the area of any autograph hunters or photographers who stupidly placed themselves in harm's way by standing in front of a fast-moving vehicle.

On one particular night we had a persistent freelance photographer with whom we'd already experienced several problems. He wasn't a fan or a collector of autographs; he operated for money, and all he wanted was pictures of Kylie, her sister Dannii or other family members as they drove out of the hotel, and he didn't really care how he obtained them. These people are classed as paparazzi, and in my opinion they're the scum of the earth. They don't care how they obtain their pictures, they don't care if people are injured in the process, nor do they care if the person they want to photograph is inconvenienced, injured or worse. This attitude seems to have been the tragic case with Princess Diana.

When Alan drove out of the loading bay that night Bill radioed me that the vehicle was on the move. Several people were at the top of the ramp, all waiting for a chance to spot Kylie. I yelled at them to keep clear, and all but the lone paparazzo moved to one side. This guy started to run backwards along the slip road, taking rapid photos as he ran in the middle of the road, flashing his camera into Alan's eyes with every picture he took. He'd obviously decided to ignore the danger of either being struck by Kylie's vehicle himself, or of his flash causing

112

Alan to swerve and hit another person. I ran after him, yelling to him to get out of the road. Needless to say he ignored me until I was standing in front of him. I felt the car literally inches from us both, and more as an instinctive move than anything else I grabbed hold of his jacket to push him to one side. He'd been anticipating this, because he brought his knee up into my stomach and slapped me across the head. As I'd been trying to stop him from getting killed I didn't class this as a fair outcome. Natural aggression took over, and in seconds we were scuffling in front of the car, which was forced to stop. Not exactly an impressive sight for Kylie and her family. Still, a few seconds later I managed to push him to one side and, with a wave of thanks, Alan drove past.

The result of all this was that I filed an assault charge against the photographer, and a court date was set. When Bill and I arrived in court (he had witnessed the incident as well as Alan and Kylie's party), we sat wondering where Alan was. We eventually sat for a couple of hours before being told that the defence counsel's car had broken down, and the court date would have to be changed! We trudged back to work, frustrated. Our second attempt ended equally frustratingly, when our prosecuting counsel realised for the second time that Alan Dallo hadn't been called as a witness. As the assault had happened directly in front of Alan's car, and had been highlighted in his headlights, this seemed unbelievable. So, even though everyone involved in the case was sitting in court waiting for it to go ahead, the whole thing was cancelled yet again. Sorry, taxpayer!

The third date was made, and before going to court I rang the witness liaison people to ensure that Alan had actually been listed and contacted as a witness. 'Oh yes,' they replied, 'of course he has. That's why the last court appearance was cancelled.' Yeah, right, how foolish of me to question you.

When Bill and I got to court I immediately checked with the officials to see if Alan had been called as a witness, and the answer was of course 'no'! At this point I stuck my heels in and refused to go into the courtroom unless Alan was present. It wasn't the best thing to do, because legally I didn't have the right to refuse, but it was accepted by the hierarchy that the CPS should have contacted Alan and that, as the leading witness, he should definitely be in court to give evidence. The case was postponed yet again, and as we left the magistrates' court for the third time without a hearing, I wondered just how many times this happened in other cases. The costs incurred by cancellation of hearings must surely be phenomenal. I had a vision of members of the CPS sitting round a bonfire of money, burning it for fun, reassuring each other with comments like, 'Oh well, let's just watch it burn, it's not our money anyway, and we won't have to drag anyone to court today. We'll just reduce the cost of the hearings to ashes and not have to disturb anyone.'

So we waited for the next date, then approximately a month later I was rushed into hospital for surgery. Just guess when the next court date was arranged! I managed to contact the court, who wanted everything in writing (when I no more felt like writing and explaining everything to them yet again than slitting my own throat). I rang Alan to see if he'd been called as a witness, and, surprise, surprise, he still hadn't heard anything from the CPS or witness liaison people.

In the end the case was thrown out. I think the judge got fed up with its repeat listing and the non-appearance of any witnesses. I put the whole thing down to the complete inefficiency of anyone connected with the CPS, and resolved my own frustrations by writing a two page letter to them in which I berated their service, attitude and incompetence. I got a phone call from them two days later to thank me for my very helpful comments! They informed me that they always welcomed and appreciated feedback from people who attended court as a witness, would certainly look into the case, and would write to me shortly with the outcome of their investigation. That was at least four years ago, and I'm still waiting.

In fairness to court officials, I'm sure they have an incredibly hard job, but they seriously need to learn how to communicate.

At one time in my career within shopping centre security, I became so fascinated with courts and their apparent inability to get anything right, that I gave up a very lucrative salary to go and work for them for a couple of months as a court security officer, just to try and understand how and why things went wrong. It was interesting for a short period of time, but I still failed to discover why our legal system continually lets down those whose faith is so blindly placed in it. Unless, of course, you go back to non-communication, inefficiency and incompetence. The system failed the public then, and I believe it still fails them now.

I remember one particularly nasty case where the whole family of the accused (the father) turned up each day to sit in the public gallery, and listened to the long list of his misdemeanours and criminal activities. At the end of the week the judge summed up the case and announced a custodial sentence. Although we had security officers and the court police officer in the gallery to ensure there were no problems during sentence, the wife of the sentenced man leapt to her feet and shouted out, 'That's not fucking justice. How can you deprive this family of their father?'

The judge, without even glancing up from his paperwork, replied slowly, 'Madam, unless you remain quiet and sit down immediately I'll deprive the family of their mother as well.' It was probably the funniest thing I've ever heard in a court – and certainly the one and only time I ever admired anyone in a court of law.

A ghost drifts in.

*The Midlands, early 1990s. I'm sitting in the witness room in a magistrates' court. It's eerily quiet. I've met the police officer who's dealing with my case. It's against a guy I've had a lot of trouble with, and I'm charging him with assault and threatening behaviour. He's just a small-time drug dealer who wants to be thought of as big-time. We've had him barred from the shopping centre but he still comes back. No doubt it boosts his morale to strut through the shops and have security officers follow him, making sure he keeps walking through to the other side and out again. We've learned to play his games, and unless he stops or causes further problems with some of his mates we merely monitor him until he leaves. He tries several times to get the ban revoked, using solicitors' letters to try and bully us into acquiescing (no doubt paid for by the taxpayer), but each time we refuse him re-entry. The attraction of the shopping centre is that it keeps him away from the eyes of the police when he carries out his drugs deals, usually conducted in corridors or toilets where there's no CCTV cover. We keep the police informed, but he's not stupid, and deals are carried out quickly and efficiently; very often by the time the police arrive he and his cronies have left. He blames me directly for being banned from the centre because I'm in charge of the security team, and I've had many run-ins with him. On several occasions I've come across him and his friends in the town centre when I've been off duty and he's gone into demented mode, screaming, swearing and shouting abuse. I no longer go into town with my family because they've also been threatened. One night when I leave to go home a man in a balaclava jumps out from behind my car, presumably to frighten me. It doesn't, and I recognise him immediately because of his body language. I use his name, and he threatens me with death before we get into the inevitable scuffle. I let the police know, tell them who I think it was, give a good description of his clothing, and describe the balaclava as looking more homemade than bought, with large stitching down the front.*

*As I sit in the witness room I become aware of someone standing outside the door. There's a clear view because most of the door is fire resistant glass. The figure is wearing a balaclava over his head with large stitching down the front, but I still recognise him as the man I'm waiting to go into court with. More to the point, I recognise the balaclava. The figure points at me, then makes a threatening, slicing motion across his throat before disappearing. I'm not sure whether to laugh or take the threat seriously. I'm sitting in a witness room in a magistrates' court for heaven's sake: where is everyone? Someone must have seen this. Apparently not. I leave the room, and walk a few steps to the police room. The door is pulled to, so I knock and go in and tell the young police officer there what has happened. Chaos ensues. Later I speak to the prosecuting counsel. She informs me that although what has occurred is intimidation of a witness, it's better if the case goes ahead. I go back to sitting and waiting, and eventually the young police officer comes back to let me know that they've found and arrested the guy, and that he had a balaclava in his pocket. It had big stitching down the front, exactly as I'd described it. Later in the day I leave court. I've not appeared as a witness, because when they brought the guy in he somehow gave the police the slip and disappeared back into the crowded city centre. It's unbelievable. Yet more unbelievable is the fact that the CPS decide they can't prosecute him for intimidation of a witness because they can't be sure that the balaclava is the same balaclava used by the guy who attacked me, and they can't be sure that the guy in court with the balaclava on his head is the same guy who attacked me that night – because of course he wore a balaclava!*

This was the first time that I began to realise there's a big difference between English law and English justice, that there's no such thing as witness protection, and that no-one is looking after Mr or Mrs Average. You have to do that yourself. You're the only person you can rely on to look after you.

My last reflection before I leave the extremely frustrating subject of law and law courts, is of a three-way triangle between HM Courts Service (HMCS), Fathers4Justice (F4J) and a Manchester hotel.

One of my final roles was to provide security cover for a Family Justice Council conference to be held at the hotel. Bill was working with me, and we had our first meeting with six HMCS security and safety officials and officers from Greater Manchester Police (GMP) early one morning. During the meeting a representative of HMCS security department confidently announced that there were no new or known threats to the judges who would be present. He then read out a recently released statement from a known activist from F4J, saying that he knew a certain judge (whom he named) was going to attend the conference, and that there was going to be, as he put it, 'a disruption of the proceedings'. Bearing in mind that the conference was to be held on the same date as the trial in Manchester (a short distance from the hotel) of a prominent member of F4J, who a month or so before I joined the hotel had disrupted a similar conference in the hotel by setting off fireworks and fire alarms, then handcuffed himself to a government minister, I unsurprisingly classed this as a threat! There was a surprised and stunned silence around the table when I made this point, followed by the comment, 'Well, yes, I suppose it is.' After this all sorts of risk assessments were carried out, and restricted emails, letters and other documents began to circulate.

Now I certainly wouldn't condemn members of F4J. I'm sure some of them have valid reasons for believing they've been treated unfairly. Nor would I dream of criticising anyone who worked in a family court, or the decision-makers who have to sift through the tragedy of broken marriages and confused children. However, I was amazed at the apparent stupidity of those tasked with the safety of those people, where the simple, most basic security requirements seemed to fail to materialise in the minds of their security personnel.

When the conference took place we ended up with at least a dozen police officers around the hotel, a helicopter circling overhead, eight additional security guards to protect all entrances and exits to the conference area, and Bill and me patrolling, checking and double-checking the conference floor and the entry and exit routes connected to it. In the end a well-known member of F4J was arrested as he walked towards the hotel from the direction of the law courts. As always, I have nothing but praise for GMP. The police officers both organising and attending the event were superb, and it's highly probable that with the exception of the buzz of the helicopter and the uniformed presence outside the hotel, guests were not even aware that such a conference was taking place.

It would be nice to end there. Bill and I were both happy with the handshake from the police officers we worked with, and with the end of conference 'thank you' that we received from the conference chairman, taking pleasure from the fact we had done our job thoroughly and professionally. However, there's always something with courts of law, or those representing them, that can reduce you to teeth-grinding frustration. This came to us in the form of a letter of thanks from the Royal Courts of Justice, London, from a Right Honourable Lord Justice, for the part we'd played in providing security cover for the conference. We should have been delighted, because no-one ever thinks to thank Security. Unfortunately the letter was sent to the hotel addressed to 'Sue Johnson and Bill Forrester (security team)'. Now I'm a Jones and Bill is a Foster, so I suppose they nearly got it right. Just not completely. Maybe, as I've said all along, this sums up our courts system. We were both grateful to the honourable gentleman for taking the trouble to write at all, and I certainly don't blame him for getting our names wrong. I just blame the system for incompetence, and an attitude that 'almost getting it right' is acceptable.

## CHAPTER TWELVE
# REBUILDS, OPENINGS AND HAUNTINGS

When a hotel in which I worked suffered a major fire, I learned two valuable lessons. One was that no matter how many times you took hotel staff through specific training it probably wouldn't get absorbed by them. This was because the sessions were more likely to be taken by the majority as an opportunity to sit down and escape the demands of a busy day, rather than a possible life-saving lesson. The second was that no matter how many modern fire alarm systems you install in hotels, if staff, guests and visitors don't know what to do when the alarms go off their chances of survival lessen considerably: the system will only ever be as effective as their response to it. I also doubt that many guests take the time to read the fire instructions on the back of their door or check for their nearest fire escape route. After all, that's someone else's responsibility, isn't it? And anyway, how could anything happen to this immaculate, modern building they've chosen to stay in? The truth is that a fire alarm warns of a fire and tells everyone to get out. If people hearing the alarm haven't taken their personal responsibility seriously, and don't know how to get out, the consequences can be fatal.

There's also a third lesson, relating to 'It'll never happen to me.' Well it can, and as statistics show it does. The problem was always going to be how to get this across to staff.

A ghost flits past, bringing with it feelings of guilt and self-recrimination.

*I'm back home after a week abroad. It's getting more and more difficult to do this job. I now have a four-year-old son, and my levels of concentration when I'm away aren't always fully on the task in hand. This could have lethal consequences. While I was out of the country the papers carried the story of a tragic house fire, and my mind wallows in the guilty thought that this might be my home one day, when I'm absent and not there to protect my young son. True, my husband is home looking after him, but what if smoke overcame him, leaving my son alone and unprotected? I hate my imagination sometimes. I come up with an ideal plan to cover this – I'll teach my four year old how to escape from a burning home, without anyone to help him. A month later and my son's nightmares are definitely diminishing! I try to soothe my guilt by knowing that at least he is now capable of getting out of his bedroom window unaided; lucky we live in a single-storey cottage.*

I push the ghosts behind me. OK, so it wasn't the best idea I ever came up with.

Anyway, the hotel that burned down had been a very attractive property. It stood on its own small island, surrounded by deep water, canal locks, barges and swans, and was joined to the mainland by a narrow bridge. It nestled just off the M53 in a quiet location, and if you wanted a peaceful hotel in close proximity to Liverpool and Manchester this would have been the hotel for you. Apart from being next to the Manchester Ship Canal, very little traffic bothered it. It breathed peace and tranquillity. Well, it did until I believe (it was never proved) someone decided to set fire to a stack of paperwork foolishly stored in the hotel's roof space. After that it became anything other than peaceful until its total refurbishment and reopening nearly twelve months later. The good thing was that nobody was hurt in the fire, probably because of the low occupancy that night. The bad thing was that eventually almost every member of staff lost their job.

On the night of the fire I arrived when the roof was well ablaze, fire engines were already pumping gallons of water from the nearby dock onto the roof, and people were walking around with glazed expressions on their faces. In a short time the fire brigade had total control of the area, the few guests we had were transferred to a sister hotel in Liverpool, and most members of staff remained huddled in the car park on the mainland side, not sure what they could do to help but unwilling to leave.

Shortly after I arrived I was approached by one of the young managers, a copy of the hotel crisis plans tucked under his arm. I clearly remember our conversation.

'Oh, thank goodness you've arrived. What's the number for the Liverpool hotel?'

I gave it to him, then looked at the folder he was carrying. 'The number's in there,' I pointed out.

'Where?' he asked, perplexed.

'In the plans you've got. The ones under your arm.' I saw enlightenment starting to dawn. 'That's why I wrote them. To take the guesswork out of a situation like this. Remember your training?'

He met my eyes sheepishly. 'I didn't look,' he admitted. 'I remembered to bring them out, but I forgot to look in them.'

'If you remember any part of your training, you'll also recall I told all managers to put names and contact numbers of the other hotels and members of the crisis team in their mobiles as well. That was so you'd never have to try to remember numbers in an emergency. This coming back to you? No? Obviously not!'

That's when my first lesson was reiterated. After each fire and evacuation training session I'd given in the hotel, I'd always repeated at the end, 'Don't forget to take your copy of the crisis plans with you.' What I should have said was, 'Don't forget to take your copy of the crisis plans with you, and when you do, OPEN AND READ THEM!' It can sometimes be difficult to recall facts in a crisis, mainly because of the psychological and physiological effects of the crisis on the human body and mind. That's why I'd written the crisis plans in the first place.

It used to be a legal requirement, and probably still is, that twice a year (three times a year for night staff) all hotel staff must be taken through fire training. Every hotel I worked in met that criterion and duly arranged the sessions. The reasons they often failed to get these sessions across to the majority of staff were mainly for the reasons I mentioned earlier. The training was frequently not taken as seriously as it should have been, and few people believed that they'd actually be involved in something like a fire – after all, hotels look so safe.

What frightened me most about hotels was that a lot of casual staff had very little knowledge of English, in some cases none at all. Because of that, the majority of hotels failed to comply with the law by not being able to train *all* staff to respond safely to fire alarms and evacuations, no matter what their paperwork said. I can hear every training manager in every hotel across the country screaming, 'But we catered for that with flash cards, having translators present, departmental training to support hotel training ...' I hear you all, but you still failed – sorry!

The housekeeping department in the majority of hotels usually had a large complement of staff from Spain and Eastern Europe, in particular Lithuania, Poland and Russia. That these ladies worked incredibly hard is beyond doubt; that their English was usually poor or non-existent is also beyond doubt.

As part of the security team duties, both day and night shifts carried out checks throughout the hotel, looking for any health, safety and security issues, making sure all fire exits were clear and that all fire-fighting equipment was in order. I also used to make regular checks on maids' trolleys, ensuring that lists bearing guest names and room numbers hadn't been left on the top of them for anyone to see. This happened on an alarmingly regular basis, and could result in undesirables illegally entering guest rooms. It wasn't unusual for thieves to make their way up onto the floors, have a quick look at the maids' trolleys, find a rooming list, then use the information about guest names and room numbers to bluff the maid into letting them into a room. This was something else we offered training against, but a confident trickster could, and often did, use an assured, assertive and sometimes aggressive approach to gain entry this way and steal valuables.

During these patrols I always stopped to speak to the girls. Some I would get to know well; some I never got to know because of the transitory nature of hotel staff; and some I ended up interviewing because of inevitable accusations by guests that money or valuables had gone missing, and the 'maid had done it'. I always had a deep respect for the majority of these maids, because of the very hard job they had to do, usually in extremely hot conditions (why does the air conditioning in hotels never work properly, if at all?) with little or no thanks. However, the number of maids who actually understood or spoke the English language frightened me then, as it does now. I never met a maid who couldn't say 'yes' or 'good morning', but that's not the point. More than one of my conversations would run something like this:

'Hi there, good morning, how are you today?'

'Yes, yes, good morning.' Lots of head-bobbing and smiles from the maid.

'Are you busy today? It looks like you've got a lot of rooms to clean this morning.'

'Yes, yes, good morning, yes.'

'Do you know we're evacuating the hotel right now because it's on fire?'

'Yes, yes, good morning.'

'Hmm, OK. Do you know what I'm saying to you?'

'Yes, yes, very busy, good morning.'

'I'm just letting you know, because you are now the only member of staff left alive in the hotel; the rest have burned to death.'

The smile by now would be growing dim, but as I moved away I'd inevitably hear, 'Yes, yes, good morning.'

Was this unfair of me? I don't think so. I'd go down to the human resource department (or inhuman remains department as a close colleague of mine used to call it), and report it all to them, They'd assure me that all members of staff, particularly maids, and specifically the maid cleaning on the floor I'd just been on, did speak English, and I'd probably just made her nervous. Right. Trust me, employing a member of staff who could neither speak nor understand English made me a lot more nervous than I ever made them!

I remember one case when the fire alarms activated, and as a guest was making her way out of her room the maid decided to try and enter, pulling her trolley across the doorway and actually preventing the guest from leaving! The guest, needless to say, was quite alarmed. I had to spend the next thirty minutes apologising to her, reassuring her that all our staff were thoroughly trained as to what they should do in the event of a fire alarm, and that of course all members of staff could speak English, even when I knew perfectly well that this wasn't true.

Anyway, back to the hotel we lost through fire. In actual fact the roof caved in not just because of the fire but also because of the amount of water the fire brigade pumped onto it; in fairness it was nothing to do with a maid's inability to speak English! This mash of water, debris, melted wires and collapsed roof then filtered through each floor, making the entire building unsafe and unstable.

So, the hotel was closed down, and I sorted out site security for the first night, knowing that stronger physical barriers would have to be put up to ensure people didn't inadvertently wander onto the land surrounding the unsafe building. Since the hotel had opened, there'd been an unwritten right adopted by a few locals that they could walk across the hotel land, because that's what they'd done before the hotel was built. There was also a New Age travellers' site not too far from the hotel, and many of these people liked to fish close to the hotel. Legally we had a responsibility to keep them all away from the site for their own safety.

After the fire I got home in the early hours of the morning, only to have my mobile phone ring. It was one of the site guards, and he was obviously upset and stressed. He also had a very broad Irish accent, and I had trouble understanding what he was saying. It became apparent that he was about to leave the site and go home – something practically unheard of from a site guard, unless he was injured or dying.

'Is it you yourself, Sue?' he asked. 'I haf to let you know I'm leaving now. Sure the place isn't fit to work in, and I'm not one for causing trouble, but there's t'ings here that would make anyone nervous and not want to stay.'

It's very unusual for a site guard to complain about a working environment. They are used to the most appalling conditions, and the guards that night had the use of a lock-keeper's hut with water, electricity and an ample supply of tea, coffee and biscuits. I know, because I'd put them in there myself.

'What's the problem?' I asked, completely baffled.

'Sure, 'tis the swans. They're never normal birds. You walk around the hotel, and the feckin' t'ings come flyin' atcha, heads all stretched, hissing and clicking their beaks, and I can't do me job while this is going on. It's not natural. 'Tis a terrible noise their wings make. They can break a man's arm, I've heard, and there's plenty of 'em around the hotel.'

I was caught off guard. 'I'm sorry ... you're leaving the site because it has swans on it?'

The Irish accent became even harder to understand. 'They're never normal birds, they come over like the divil himself. Sure, they're vicious, and when they're not flying atcha, b'Jesus they're runnin' atcha, their tails twitching, and their necks all arched, and they've got red eyes. I'm not stayin', and I'm sorry I'm lettin' you down, but it's not right to have to walk around the hotel and never know which direction they're comin' from. It's a bad omen, that an' the hotel burnin' an' all. To have such a t'ing on the first night, no, it's not right. Goodbye.' And that was it – he left!

The following day I walked around the hotel, and sure enough a couple of swans were nesting across the water on the other side of one of the docks. They watched me with interest, but when it was obvious I wasn't going to be a threat they ignored me. I wondered what the Irish guy had done to upset them so much, or if there was another reason behind his rapid departure. Before too long I was to find out.

My mobile rang a few weeks later. It was after midnight, and I'd just climbed into bed. It was the new site guard, and I wondered for a second if I was about to lose another guard to the 'devil swans'. 'I'm just letting you know that I've seen torchlight moving on the second floor of the hotel, and it's supposed to be empty … I'm on my own, because the other guy hasn't turned up yet, and I'm not going in there on my own. Anyway, we aren't allowed in because of Health and Safety.' He drew breath long enough for me to reply.

'OK, just monitor it, and I'll come over.'

'Do you want me to call the police?' he asked.

'No.'

The guards had been seeing lights in the hotel since the very first night. I'd called the police out on two previous occasions, but after a detailed search nothing had been found. In fairness, the hotel had become a building site, the responsibility of the builders, and officially the guards shouldn't have been going in there, but the lights and the fact that the police hadn't been able to find anyone had without doubt spooked them.

As I pulled on an old pair of jeans and a jumper, the issue of the lights began to run through my mind. To my knowledge there was no longer an electricity supply to the hotel, so the only source of light had to be a torch. The whole area was sealed off with metal sheeting, but I knew as well as the guards did that this didn't offer complete protection from anyone determined enough to want to gain entry. I was sure there was a simple explanation to it all.

I've never been nervous about going into empty buildings, or searching large, deserted areas; part of my early training, I suppose. But the problems I'd been having in Liverpool with a couple of notorious gangsters made me just a bit more wary. Boyd and Shaun had been working with me at the site to get it secured, and I knew Boyd could get there quite quickly. I gave him a call and asked him to meet me at the hotel.

We both arrived approximately forty minutes later. I pulled the car onto the rough ground overlooking the hotel on the mainland side, switched the lights off, and when Boyd joined me in my car we sat looking out over the deserted building. I'd been able to see lights in the lock-keeper's hut, but had known they would belong to the security guard. The hotel itself was in total darkness.

'How long are we waiting?' Boyd asked. I sensed his unease at doing nothing. Boyd was an action man; inactivity had never appealed to him.

'Let's just give it a few more minutes, to get a feel of the place and see if anyone's moving around before we go in,' I suggested.

I'd hardly spoken before we saw the quick flash of a light on the third floor. Boyd reached for the door handle, but I caught his arm. 'Just wait. Just a few seconds more. Let's see if it moves about.'

Understanding Boyd's desire to get going, we went through how we'd get into the building and make our way up the floors. I knew the hotel inside out. I also knew there was a loose lock on the kitchen window at the back of the hotel, because despite many reminders to the builders I guessed they wouldn't have fixed it.

The light showed again, this time further to the right. Whoever it was, they were moving around.

'OK, let's go. No torches, no speaking, no noise. I'll go first. You follow me.'

'No. I'll go first, you follow me.' I was about to respond with a scathing remark about this not being the time for gallantry when Boyd continued, 'Give me your baton.'

'What?'

'Your baton. Give it to me.'

'Why are you going to have it?'

'Because I'm going in first.'

'What if he or they appear behind me?' I started to ask, but Boyd was already holding out his hand. We paused in our seats, scanning the hotel for any further sight of the light. I didn't need the baton anyway, as I had another one, but I kept that information to myself. I didn't want Boyd going in with both batons swinging!

So, muttering about it being illegal to carry them, and that if the police caught him with it he could explain, I reached into the car door pocket for the familiar cold steel. I found it beneath what felt like several chocolate wrappers and something gooey. I really had to clean the car out, I thought, as I handed the baton over. Both our eyes were still fixed on the front windows of the hotel.

'Oh my God! That's so disgusting!' Boyd suddenly said.

'What? What is? Where?' 'I asked, looking everywhere for the reason for this outburst.

'There.' For the life of me I still couldn't see the reason for his exclamation.

'Boyd, where? Where are you looking?' I started to get annoyed that I still couldn't see anything out of the ordinary.

'There, on top of your baton.' Boyd gesticulated in the moonlight to its very tip. A piece of well-mouthed chewing gum sat resplendent on the small round metal top. 'You're so disgusting. I can't believe you treat this baton like that.'

I started to push him out of the car. 'I treat the whole car like that; it's practically a mobile home.' I dropped my voice to a whisper. 'Hush now and stop fussing: you're making enough noise to wake the dead.'

We made our way quietly to the back of the hotel, following the path alongside the large deep dock, hoping we couldn't be seen by anyone inside the hotel. I found the loose lock, and slowly moved to unlock it with a small pocket knife I always carried with me. Then, without warning, absolute hell broke loose behind us.

I can only describe the sound as a mini-explosion of water and high -pitched screaming. I thought a small submarine was surfacing behind us. Boyd's language was explosive and unrepeatable, mine no better. Whatever it was, it was moving quickly towards us across the water, and it sounded like the hounds of hell had been unleashed. I still don't know how Boyd made it through the window. He's a big guy, standing at least six foot three. He made it through in record time, and I wasn't far behind him. I don't know who made more noise, the water banshee or us.

From the safety of the deserted kitchen we peered back through the window. Two enormous swans were inches from the path we'd just walked down. The noise had been the furious beating of their wings on water as they propelled themselves across the dock, hissing and screeching. They must have heard us when we first started walking round the hotel, and decided we were just too close to their nest on the other side of the dock. If ever I might have suffered a heart attack that was the time. I've never heard swans make such a noise before or since.

'Well, I guess that's our cover blown,' I managed to say.

Boyd's answer was yet another string of obscenities.

We searched the hotel from top to bottom, and found nothing. As Boyd pointed out, at least the back of the hotel was well protected by the swans! Presumably their reaction to anyone walking around that area at night would have been the same as their reaction to us.

We never did find out what caused those lights. The builders assured me they'd got no lights on that floor, didn't even have a power supply to that floor yet, and that there was nothing that could cause lights to go on and off in the way we described. It remained a mystery. I changed the site guarding company shortly afterwards, and the new guards also reported seeing lights every now and then. They'd investigated – and also got attacked by the swans! The mystery was never cleared up.

I'm not a believer in ghosts, apart from those I carry with me. But working at nights in properties that were either brand new or extremely old, there were often incidents I couldn't explain. You had two ways of looking at them. Either you believed that something sinister and spooky lurked around every corner, or you said to yourself, 'Get a grip! You may not know the reason for this, but I bet there's a perfectly good one – you just haven't thought of it yet.'

There was only one exception: one night probably about twenty years ago. It wasn't a hotel this time, but a shopping centre in the Midlands where I worked. The property was opened to a deadline, which inevitably meant that not all the things which should have been completed before opening were actually finished. The result was that after six months various problems kept cropping up, and workmen had to come in after the centre was closed to put things right. This meant that a security officer had to be on duty overnight to oversee everything. Part of the side of the shopping centre backed onto a very old church and churchyard, and rumour had it that some of the graves had been dug up in order to fit the shopping centre in. This led to all sorts of spooky stories of unexplained noises, false intruder activations and interruption to the CCTV system. Still, most of the lads appreciated the overtime, and there was never a shortage of volunteers to cover these shifts. To be fair to everyone I drew up a rota so they could all cover the extra night hours, usually before their day off. The workload was simple, so it only ever needed one guy at a time. They were there when the workmen arrived, signed them in, read the riot act on health and safety, checked permits to work, checked the work area after they finished, then locked the centre up again when they'd left – usually a couple of hours before opening the next day. It couldn't have been simpler. Because of this, I was surprised when one of the guys said I could take his name off the rota because he wasn't interested in covering the shift any more. I teased him, asking if he was concerned about losing beauty sleep, and was surprised when he replied, 'No, I just don't like ghosts.' I laughed, only to discover he was deadly serious. Eventually, with several nervous laughs, he told me about the shopping centre ghost.

The centre had been opened in two stages. Phase One, which opened out into the town centre, was part of a listed building and a much older construction than its Phase Two counterpart. Because of this many of its original features had been kept as part of the shopping complex. Just inside the front doors the roof reached up into an arched atrium, and at the top of the winding stone stairs leading to the atrium, the security team had been allocated a rest room, where they could brew a coffee, have lunch and generally relax while on a break. It wasn't particularly comfortable but it provided the basics of a table, half a dozen chairs, a microwave and a toaster. The main door was big and solid, and when shut it kept in a lot of noise (not that we made much), so shoppers passing below weren't disturbed. The only other way in was through the rear door, which was accessed via second-floor service corridors. It gave us a lot of privacy, and compared with a lot of places I've worked, it was wonderful.

The security lad in question, I'm going to call him John, seemed sincere about his concerns. I later found out that most of the team had experienced similar events; they just weren't as honest in coming forward. Anyway, John had been on duty one night while contractors were working at the back of the centre, the opposite end to Phase One. He did a complete round to make sure that all was secure, all doors were locked and that the contractors were OK, then walked through the main shopping centre to Phase One to make himself a cup of coffee in the rest room. As he turned the corner towards the front roller-shutter, he heard a noise from the atrium above him. It surprised him because, with the exception of himself and the workmen he'd just checked at the other end of the centre, no-one should have been there. Thinking that there might be an intruder, he stopped and listened, and heard a sound like a chair being scraped back. Then, he said, 'everything went mad'. It sounded as if two men were fighting, overturning chairs and table; this was no silent intruder! Being practical, and believing that somehow at least two people had got into the rest room, John bravely lunged through the door out of Phase One, and up the winding stairs towards the rest room. As he ran up the stairs he said the noise was incredible and he was sure he was going to be breaking up a fight. Being fit, it probably took him no more than thirty seconds to reach the heavy wooden door that blocked his way into the room, and then he stopped dead. The noise inside had ceased. There was complete silence. Concerned that whoever was in there would escape through the back door, he charged in and skidded to a halt. There was nobody there. The table and chairs were upright and neat, and there was absolutely no sign of any disturbance. That's when he said he freaked.

After this incident there were several other reports of peculiar goings-on. Tenants reported hearing odd things when they shut up their shops at night, and a couple of shop staff reported bumps and bangs in Phase One, usually early in the morning or late at night.

There's nothing worse than an active imagination, fed regularly by scary tales. Before long the lads were finding excuses for not carrying out additional hours after closing, particularly if this involved working all night. I teased them relentlessly (as they had always teased me if I messed up), with the obvious result that guess who did the next nightshift ... It did occur to me at the time that I was probably being set up! I had believed John when he'd told me the story, but given the choice of believing a team of guys who couldn't wait to see me fall flat on my face or believing in aggressive ghosts, I chose the set-up. It didn't matter either way, because the wonderful thing about working in a shopping centre that's closed to the public is that it gives you time to complete the dreaded paperwork.

So that night I stayed behind, and said goodnight to the last security officer as he went home. I booked in the contract team as they arrived, and carried out the usual checks and logs. Then, because I was absolutely sure that a set-up was planned, I went round every door, every shutter, and double-checked that the centre was completely locked and closed down. Then, isolating the intruder system where the contractors were working, I switched on the rest of the system. If anyone so much as breathed outside the corridor the men were in I'd know about it. In fact, because of the noise the alarms made, half the town centre would hear about it! I completed my paperwork, and had a coffee in the centre manager's kitchen (sorry about that: your office was nearer than Phase One and I didn't want to turn the intruder system off again!). I checked all the cameras regularly, but nothing moved. I couldn't see the contractors because they were working in a service corridor that wasn't covered by CCTV, but any movement outside their area would set off the alarms.

It was bliss to work in such silence. And I guessed I was wrong about the set-up, because midnight came and went, then 1am and 2am, and all was silent and still. The workmen finished at about 2.30am, and I turned off the alarms, let them all out onto the loading bay, and raised the huge roller-shutter for them to go home. No problems. I brought the shutter down, and checked the corridor where they had been working. All was well. I was about to start shutting down the security control room to go home myself, when I realised I couldn't remember locking the service corridor door. Annoyed at my stupidity I locked the control room, then walked down the stairwell and through the door onto the loading bay. I cursed because it had started to rain heavily and I hadn't brought a coat with me. I put my head down and ran across the wide bay to the door at the other side. I gave it a quick test to make sure it was actually locked, and began to turn to run back. Then I heard a noise. To this day I couldn't tell you what it was, but it wasn't a shopping centre noise. It sounded human, but it was distant and indistinct. I'd checked all the contractors in and checked the same number out, but I suddenly wondered if someone had found a way into the centre that none of us knew about. It was also possible that a member of shop staff had remained behind, deciding for some reason to stay in the centre all night. Whoever it was they couldn't move far, because all corridors were locked with master keys and very few people apart from me, the centre manager and the maintenance manager had one. For a brief second I wondered if this was the beginning of the set-up I had expected, but it didn't make sense to hold it here. None of the lads would have expected me to double-check this area. Anyway, set-up, intruder or not, I knew I had to check out the sound.

I took the master key off my bunch and, as silently as I could, unlocked the door. I moved quickly into the murky darkness of the service corridor, shutting and locking the door as if it were cracked glass, then stood, listening carefully. There was no sound at all. The corridor I'd walked onto was on the second floor of the shopping centre, so as quietly as I could I made my way over to the top of the nearby stairwell, then listened for at least five minutes for any sound either along the corridor I was on, or from the floor below me. But there was nothing. I could hear the wind blowing outside and rain lashing against the door I'd just come through, but that was it. Against one of the emergency exit signs I could see that the dust the contractors had disturbed when they'd been working was settling again, but apart from my own wet footprints from the loading bay there was no indication that anyone else was around. Then I heard it again: a faint sound from the floor below. Very slowly I began to make my way down the dimly lit stairwell, illuminated only by the emergency lighting system. I had leather soled shoes on, and they made no sound on the concrete stairs. I reached the bottom and stopped to listen once more. Then, this time from the floor above, the one I'd just left, I heard another noise: again something alien to the normal sounds of a shopping centre, even an empty one. Mouth open, I strained to listen, and heard what sounded like a key in the door I'd walked through a few minutes earlier, then, weirder still, the quick click of a woman's heeled boots on the flooring above me. I listened to at least six or seven confident, clear steps, and then I sprinted up the stairs towards her. I slowed only as I reached the next floor; it was almost a relief to be facing someone. Except that when I looked down the length of the corridor, and then towards the door I'd heard open, there was absolutely nobody there at all. Imagination? I don't think so. I immediately checked the door leading out onto the loading bay, the one I'd heard being unlocked. It was locked, and there were no prints to indicate that anyone other than I had been there since the contractors. There was no explanation for it at all – but I never teased the lads again when they reported ghostly happenings at night.

I think there are always tales of strange goings on when a new hotel first opens. Staff aren't used to the building, and there's always some sort of movement and settlement that goes on for months, creating an ideal environment for scary stories. Sometimes the opening of a new hotel created situations that you wouldn't believe possible if you sat down and made them up! The opening of a hotel in Liverpool in the late 1990s was a good example of this.

The VIP list for the opening ceremony was impressive. It included Frankie Vaughan, who was going to cut the red tape, the Lord Mayor of Liverpool, the Lord Mayor of Dublin, and mayors from Sefton, Knowsley, St Helens and Wirral. Apart from my usual duties of checking that all arrivals and departures were going to run smoothly, and that no-one was going to upset the operational proceedings or attempt to assassinate any of the attending VIPs, I didn't really have a lot to do on the day. However, the Lord Mayor of Dublin had announced that he must get to Manchester Airport quite quickly after the ceremony, in order to catch a flight back to Ireland to attend another official function. With his usual flair, the hotel's owner had arranged for a helicopter to come and pick him up after the opening ceremony. It was to land on rough ground near the docks, as close to the hotel as the law would allow, and I got the job of driving the mayor to the waiting helicopter. Time was of the essence if he was to catch his Manchester flight, so his schedule was tight.

Just to make sure that I didn't get lost driving from the hotel to the correct dock, I made a few dummy runs before the big day arrived. At the last moment it was decided (probably quite rightly) that my car was a disgrace, and that no self-respecting mayor should be asked to travel in it. It was agreed that I should drive the car belonging to the owner's personal assistant, which was much more luxurious – and clean! No problem: how could anything go wrong?

The opening ceremony went well. I collected the PA's car: it felt like luxury to step into such a clean vehicle, all warmed up ready with the engine running for me. As the mayor said his farewells to the other dignitaries, I sedately drove the car round to the front of the hotel to meet him.

What a nice guy he was. He was chatting to me even before he settled himself into the front passenger seat (I'd expected him to get into the back!), and by the time we'd sorted seatbelts out, disentangled the gold chain from the belt buckle and removed part of his coat from the car door, we were ready to move. I slowly pulled out of the hotel grounds and drove towards the Mersey and the complex layout of docks and dirt tracks that at the time passed for roads. We chatted all the way. As we drove the mayor took off his chain of office, but before he put it in its official-looking box he started to explain all about it. He really was a lovely man. By the time my education about the chain and its history had finished, I was driving onto the extremely small landing area, where the helicopter was waiting. I was quite surprised to see two police cars parked there, but pleased too: it gave the mayor a fitting send-off.

There was very little space for the helicopter to have landed in, and an equally small amount of space for me to park in. Unfortunately the two police cars took up quite a bit of the limited land to my right, the helicopter monopolised the ground to my left, and there was an extremely deep dock in front of me. I was left with the decision of either parking quite a way from both helicopter and police vehicles (making the mayor walk through mud and potholes) or to drive up under the helicopter blades (currently stationary), which would delay his take-off until I moved the car. At that moment the beautiful gold chain slid off the mayor's knee and disappeared onto the floor somewhere near his feet. Thinking of time, and that I'd probably have to get the mayor out of the car before we could retrieve the chain, I decided to drive as close to the helicopter as possible, park, extract the mayor, find and box the gold chain, then reverse away from the helicopter before the pilot started up the blades.

And it would have all worked out too, except for the fact that I wasn't driving my own car. Not being a car person, it never occurred to me (nor had anyone pointed it out) that once the engine was stopped, an immobiliser kicked in and you needed a code to restart it.

So I stopped the car under the rotor blades, turned off the engine because I was literally only a few feet from the unprotected dock, then walked round to the mayor's side. I extracted his chain, and there was a certain amount of thanks, handshaking, and the waving of gratitude to the police cars, before the mayor climbed into the helicopter, the pilot all the while glancing at his watch. I ran back to the car, got in and turned the key in the ignition. I know now why it wouldn't start, but at the time I thought fate had taken the opportunity to give me a good kick while it had the chance. The pilot of course couldn't start his blades moving because the car was so close, and the police drivers (both of whom I knew) looked as if they were about to die laughing.

In the end the police and I managed by pure brute force to move the car sideways towards their vehicles, with enough space for the pilot to think he could safely lift the helicopter up. It probably wasn't safe at all, but by this time he was a desperate man, I was a desperate woman, and the police officers were too purple in the face and short of breath to consider that a breach of aviation regulations had taken place. The mayor smiled graciously all the way through it!

So much for the opening of hotels and shopping centres.

# CHAPTER THIRTEEN
# SUICIDES, ACCIDENTS AND INJURIES

Using a hotel should be a very happy, relaxed and enjoyable experience. The whole ethos of the five star hotel is that your every whim and desire is catered for. For example, a general manager I worked for would not put tea trays in bedrooms because he believed that if anyone wanted tea or coffee they shouldn't have to make it themselves, they should pick up the phone and ask for it to be brought to them. In theory this worked really well. It certainly did when he was general manager, the hotel had a full complement of staff and all room service staff were professionals, completely dedicated to their role. Unfortunately, the dramatic reduction in staff and standards brought in by a new general manager after he left meant that this service couldn't be kept up: there just weren't enough staff to supply the demands of thirsty (or hungry) guests within the time allowed.

Like most things associated with hotels, the truth concerning their operation and service standards is often far removed from the glossy brochures or cleverly worded advertisements. Sadly, the reality of hotels is that they can be very lonely and extremely depressing places, and this can lead to all sorts of problems for guests and staff alike.

Suicide is not something you expect as part of an average day, but unfortunately sometimes it does happen. In a couple of cases I dealt with, guests had actually gone to the hotel with the intention of committing suicide. In other instances depression or mental breakdowns occurred after they checked into the hotel. Sometimes alcohol was the reason emotions tipped over into tragedy, sometimes it was drugs. But sometimes there was no apparent reason why a guest would be driven to take, or try to take, their life. We'd never find out.

Shortly before I joined a hotel in London, a young man threw himself off the roof, twenty-three floors up. The member of staff who found him handled the situation with great dignity and courage, despite the appalling tragedy of a lost life, and the manner in which it was taken. He later told me that he was 'OK about handling it' until he rang 999 to report the incident. The emergency operator apparently asked him to turn the body over to make sure the person was dead. He said that at this point he lost it completely, became hysterical, and couldn't stop laughing at the stupidity of the request. It wasn't a matter of thinking the situation was at all funny; it was just his mind's way of dealing with the tragedy, and releasing his suppressed emotions.

In another seemingly senseless act a member of a health club attached to another hotel where I worked came into the club, had a work-out, returned to her car, which was parked close to the unprotected water's edge of a deep dock, engaged first gear, then calmly drove over the lip of the dock, straight into the water. For a short while her vehicle floated, and staff and members of the club shouted at her to get out of the car while she could, but she merely wound her window down and laughed as the vehicle sank. I still think about her, and wonder at what point reality hit her, if at all, and whether she had any last-minute thoughts that could only ever come too late.

It seems so depressing to talk about suicide, particularly when you consider the hilariously funny things that can happen in a hotel. But tragedy is also unfortunately part of a hotel's varied life. Still, I'd like to think that because of the experience of handling suicide, it made me, and other members of staff, more aware of the guests who checked in, all of us hoping to reduce such acts by greater awareness and vigilance. This included noticing the guest with no luggage, or the guest who appeared depressed, withdrawn or sad. When you work with people day in, day out, for years at a time you learn to read body language and mannerisms. Team co-operation across the hotel worked well, with reception, housekeeping and cleaning staff all contributing by supplying information about a guest who was not acting 'normally'. There were certainly a couple of occasions when I was passed information about a guest who was out of the ordinary, or who seemed different from other guests. In some cases, of course, this information hinged around criminal activity, and on occasion even terrorist activity, but sometimes when I investigated I found a very unhappy or depressed guest whose intention was to take their life.

Sadly, we failed to prevent a suicide in a Manchester hotel because the problem was only suspected by the lady's husband, who unfortunately wasn't with her. By the time we were contacted, a member of the room service staff had already found her dead in her room.

Sometimes there's a build-up to a tragedy, certain actions, behaviour or comments that indicate all is not well, and signify a cry for help, even if it's not an obvious one. This was certainly true when I worked in another Manchester hotel. I was acting duty manager, and was busy dealing with several complaints from guests who were unhappy with the service they were receiving. During the morning a member of the housekeeping team rang to inform me that a guest was behaving in an odd and unusual manner in his room. As I'd just received a complaint from a guest concerning a man on the same floor, I put two and two together and went up to investigate. When I got out of the lift the young man concerned was sitting on the floor in his boxer shorts, wearing only one shoe and appeared to be very distressed about something. I asked him which room he was staying in, and when he gave me the same room number as the housekeeper had, it confirmed that this was the same person. The guest appeared completely unaware of where he was, so I persuaded him to return to his room with me. When we arrived he informed me that he'd taken an overdose, showed me letters he'd written to various people apologising for what he was about to do, and said he'd no money to pay for anything. Now this has happened to me several times before, usually with a guest who's drunk, drugged or just trying to cheat the hotel of the money they owe for their stay. But this guy was different: I got the impression he was a really nice person who was going through a very bad phase, and I was seriously concerned for his safety. I contacted the emergency services and, professional as always, they arrived and took him to hospital. But there was a follow-up to this story. The guy was obviously bothered that he couldn't pay the bill he'd run up, and I heard later from the paramedics that this had been his main topic of conversation while they were looking after him. Rightly or wrongly, I told them (as I later told him myself over the phone) he shouldn't worry about this, I'd ensure his bill was wiped off, and he should forget it. But later that day I was contacted by his parents, two lovely people, who informed me that their son had been going through a really bad patch and that he'd gone to the hotel to take his life. They also said that following his desperate act and time in hospital he now wanted to seek the help he needed, and he really, really, wanted to pay his bill. I had tremendous respect both for the guest and his parents. In the end he paid in small instalments; not because the hotel requested it but because he felt better doing it. Now that impressed me, and I was grateful to his parents for keeping me updated on how he was getting on.

On occasion we dealt with people who booked into the hotel and then, for no apparent reason, underwent a serious character change. This happened when I was in Liverpool. A young lady, Samantha, had booked in for her company's annual dinner dance. Again, it was one of the housekeepers who raised the alarm. Samantha's colleague had knocked on the door to see how she was getting on, but had received no answer. Concerned, she asked a maid to go into the room and make sure everything was OK. The maid discovered the young lady in the bathroom, talking gibberish and refusing to come out. During the next hour of trying to coax her out of the bathroom, we discovered that if we called her Sam she became childlike, and if we called her Samantha she changed into someone else. It was very distressing for all concerned. Her colleagues didn't want paramedics called, but because we were concerned that she might self-harm they finally agreed for the hotel doctor to come and assess her. In the meantime, having dressed in a maid's uniform, I managed to persuade Samantha to come out of the bathroom, and she was happily helping me make beds when the doctor arrived. Unfortunately she was sectioned under the Mental Health Act but a couple of years later I bumped into one of her colleagues and she informed me that Samantha had made a complete recovery. That had been really good news.

Something hotels have on a regular basis is accidents. Of course at Christmas and New Year there's a sharp rise in these owing to the excess of alcohol consumed. Festive accidents that I dealt with ranged from simple slips, trips and falls, to a guest (not sober) who decided to race, full pelt, down a disabled ramp, pushing a wheelchair occupied by his elderly father (sober). They ended up in a tangled and bloody mess at the bottom.

Accidents in hotel car parks were frequent, with intoxicated guests trying to vie with vehicles for right of way (and losing). Or, rather than following the pedestrian pathways, they'd take a short cut under car park barriers, not stopping to make sure they were fully raised or, worse, on the way down. The results were inevitable. We also had drivers trying to tailgate other vehicles off the car park in order to save money. Often both vehicles ended up damaged, and both drivers inevitably tried to find someone to blame other than themselves.

These events were naturally very funny for the stupefied people concerned until they saw blood or the damage they'd caused, and then it wasn't very funny any more: oh, and guess what, it was all the hotel's fault.

Someone once said that alcohol is deaf, and I know exactly what they meant. A drunken whisper usually carries a long way, and is heard by just about everyone within earshot. This can have advantages and disadvantages. Disadvantages because if your drunken whisper's detrimental about someone standing within earshot the result could end up being physical – as several guests at parties found out! On the other hand, the advantage is that an injured drunk is usually honest about his or her injuries, and very vocal about what they're going to do about it.

For example, a female guest at a party insisted on dancing in a cordoned section of the dance floor, coned off because of drinks spilled by other revellers. She ignored the fact that the area was cordoned off, she ignored the 'Danger Wet Floor' signs, and she ignored requests by hotel staff to dance in a dry section. In the end, of course, she slipped and fell. Not deterred, she laughed loudly while other guests came to her aid and attempted to lift her off the floor, then laughed even louder when their efforts resulted in them slipping as well. The manager in charge of the event was on the verge of putting up the lights and stopping the event when three guests fell together with a loud crash. The woman who'd caused all the trouble lay groaning on the floor, complaining that she couldn't move because she'd hurt her back. By the time I got there a crowd of well-wishers had gathered, offering advice and trying to drag her onto her feet – not the best thing to do with a back injury. I moved them away, suggested she didn't try to move and told her I'd call an ambulance. This hadn't gone down well either with the injured woman or her husband, who was equally inebriated, and I'd received scathing remarks about not going to hospital to wait for hours in an A&E unit before seeing someone. Despite my warning not to move her, the man dragged his wife off the floor and dumped her clumsily onto a nearby chair, before demanding a wheelchair. I suggested again that we should get professional help, and once more advised against moving her – but when the husband became increasingly loud and aggressive I asked a member of staff to bring a wheelchair up. My suggestion not to move the casualty from chair to wheelchair was met by more abuse, so I stood back and let them get on with it. The woman was deposited unceremoniously into the wheelchair by her husband, howling with pain, clutching her back and screaming that she'd sue the hotel for every penny it had. She continued to refuse to allow me to send for paramedics, so I asked if they'd like help pushing the wheelchair to a taxi. This was met with further screams: she wasn't going anywhere until she'd seen a paramedic. Even her husband looked confused at this point ... Eventually I called an ambulance. I have tremendous respect for the ambulance service, and all paramedics in that service. I particularly admire their patience when dealing with self-imposed injuries caused by excessive alcohol intake, but twenty minutes after their arrival I could see this patience was running out. The lady was drunkenly whispering to her friends that she wasn't actually injured at all but that she was going to get every penny she could out of the hotel. There were drunken whispers back, assuring her that as it was a five star hotel she'd make a lot of money.

In the end the paramedics couldn't do anything for her because she refused to go to hospital, and when she got cross with them she actually got out of the wheelchair, walked across the floor, and screamed, 'Look, I can't walk because of the pain I'm in.' The paramedics left shortly afterwards! I retrieved the wheelchair and left them to it. A couple of days later the general manager received a letter complaining about my lack of assistance, the appalling service they received from the ambulance service and the hotel's total lack of interest in what was now a disabling injury. After several letters threatening legal action, the whole thing died a death.

Because every member of the security team was first aid trained, we were always first port of call when an accident or injury occurred. I was lucky with the team of lads I worked with: there probably wasn't an injury they hadn't seen, including stab wounds and gunshot wounds. But even so, we had a few bizarre accidents that even they hadn't come across before.

I was working one night with a colleague, Steve McGee, an experienced doorman who was also a martial artist, so we had a lot in common. Steve and I always used to joke about being on shift together because there'd always be an incident or accident, and being the most experienced first aiders we'd end up mopping blood or binding broken bones until the paramedics arrived. This certainly proved to be true the day Tony Blair, then prime minister, came to visit a Liverpool hotel, but more about that later.

Anyway, this particular night we had held an event in the function suite, which seemed to go quite well. Halfway through the evening, though, we became aware that one of the guests, a man in a wheelchair, had become more and more inebriated. Now I have a very close friend who uses a wheelchair, and I know from travelling quite extensively with her in Canada that unless operated by a sane and sober person, wheelchairs can be tricky things to manoeuvre. Unfortunately, as the evening progressed it became clear that the occupant of this particular chair was neither of those things. Eventually something had to be said to the event organisers, because we'd received too many complaints about the behaviour of their disabled guest, mainly from young women. However, when I spoke to the organisers I was surprised to find that the wheelchair user was nothing to do with the party, and that they'd been on the verge of coming to see me!

The end result was that I went and spoke to the man, who by then was extremely drunk: he had been sick down the front of his shirt and become incontinent. Because of his behaviour and unwillingness to act responsibly, I didn't believe his disability was a factor that should be considered. I warned him that no further alcohol would be served to him, adding that as he wasn't a member of the party he wouldn't be allowed back in the function again. This didn't go down particularly well: he accused me of picking on him because he was disabled, and retorted that he'd be going to the papers the following day to show what sort of hotel it really was. Even though I was able to imagine my conversation with the general manager the following day about evicting a disabled person, it didn't seem fair that he should be allowed to get away with drunken behaviour on the grounds that he was disabled.

I gave him a final warning about his behaviour in the hotel, and he went off into the lounge area, where I hoped he'd sober up a bit. I wasn't so lucky. Before long we received a more serious complaint from a female guest, and as far as I was concerned this amounted to sexual assault. Regardless of his disability, that just wasn't acceptable.

So I spoke to him for the last time, telling him his behaviour was unacceptable and that I now had to ask him to leave the hotel. He instantly became abusive. I asked if he was with anyone, or whether he'd come by car, because he really wasn't in a fit state either to be on his own or to drive. When he told me that he'd come from a night out in the centre of town and that he'd go back there, I was seriously alarmed. My mind flashed up the next morning's newspaper headlines: 'Disabled man thrown out of Liverpool's leading hotel, and mugged in city centre.' Sometimes you just can't win. I offered to ring a member of his family to come and collect him, but he was having none of it, and was determined to continue into the city centre – at least a mile away. I thought about his disability and wheelchair, and asked myself a harsh question: if he wasn't disabled and he wasn't in a wheelchair, what would you do? The equally harsh answer was inevitable: I'd throw him out, and not care where he went next.

In the end he settled the problem for me by wheeling himself to the front doors of the hotel and demanding to be let out. Steve looked at me, seeking clarification that this was what we should be doing. We couldn't have kept him in the hotel against his will; there'd been several complaints about him; and he was extremely drunk. Anyone else would have been evicted hours ago. I nodded to Steve to unlock the doors and let him out, then went to phone the local police to inform them of the situation, and see if they could intervene to get him back home safely.

A few seconds later, before my phone call had even been connected, Steve radioed to say that instead of wheeling himself over the road towards the city centre, the lad had gone round the back of the hotel to the car park. This had put him in a position of danger not just to himself but to drivers entering and leaving the area. I took a quick look at the cameras to see where he'd gone, and was just in time to see his wheelchair topple off the path. Both he and his chair immediately disappeared behind a large van. I swore loudly, grabbed Steve, then both of us ran round the side of the hotel.

We found where he'd parted company with his wheelchair, because it was lying in the road on its side, but there was absolutely no sign of its occupant. Both Steve and I looked around the immediate area without success, and the thought crossed my mind; was this guy actually disabled, or had we been dealing with an able-bodied person posing as a disabled person? It had happened to me in the past. Had the guy picked himself up and run off? But the back of the hotel was protected by a high metal fence that I'd have defied an Olympic athlete to scale in the time involved: he couldn't have gone that way.

We stood for a few seconds looking around at the high-sided vans that had brought the equipment for the event that night. Then we both had the same idea. 'No, he couldn't have.' But we got down on our hands and knees anyway and peered under the nearest vehicles. The bases of those wagons were sitting so close to the ground that I thought it was a stupid idea even as I grazed my knee getting down. I'm quite short, but I doubted I could get underneath them, and Steve, who despite his six foot frame and broad shoulders was relatively slim, obviously thought the same: we both got up, not believing it was possible for anyone to fit underneath. But when we bent down once more to check another vehicle, we heard the sound of vomiting coming from beneath it.

'I don't believe it,' Steve said, before we started worming our way under the wagon to try and reach him. I caught my jacket on something, and wondered what on earth we'd look like when we got the guy out; then the smell of vomit, urine and faeces hit me full in the face and I gagged. I heard Steve doing the same as he reached to try and drag the man towards him. To this day I don't know how we got him out. He was unconscious, absolutely unable to help us, and completely wedged on his back underneath the van. I paused long enough to radio the lads, telling them we needed an ambulance, and to stand by because we might also need the fire brigade. But by some superhuman effort Steve managed to dislodge the guy, and we were able to drag him out, clear his mouth and airway of vomit, ensure he was breathing, then place him in the recovery position until the paramedics arrived.

We never did find out anything about him. He remained a mystery man from then until now. I fully understood his need for independence and control of his own life, but I felt for a long time that the least he could have done was contact the hotel to thank Steve. I certainly wouldn't have been able to move him without Steve, and I genuinely believe he'd have choked on his own vomit before the paramedics arrived if Steve hadn't been there.

Another bizarre incident occurred when Boyd Fullerton and I were working together one night in a city centre hotel. It had been a hot summer night and now it was a hot, stuffy, early morning. It must have been around 2am, because the number of drunks walking past the hotel or trying to get in to use the toilets had quadrupled. The streets were crowded because the nightclubs had closed their doors, throwing a mêlée of drunken people into the streets to try to make their way home. Most town centres would be the same on a summer night. Youngsters were hot, so they drank more in a shorter time. Unfortunately it wouldn't be water they drank, but alcopops, or shorts washed down by alcopops, beer or any other cold, fizzy, alcoholic drinks. Because they had a time limit in which to 'enjoy' themselves and stay cool at the same time, the result was inevitable. Drunken kids no longer in control of themselves, fights, rapes, vomiting, urinating and defecating in the street, and the inevitable trips to A&E ... Here the already overworked staff would try to ensure that the human being once present in that wreck of a body was restored, ready to do it all again the next weekend. I suppose that's why I have such a tremendous respect for paramedics and nursing staff. Having to deal with aggressive, drunken, stinking people who arrived in that condition through their own actions surely wasn't on their nursing job descriptions; not to mention the number of assaults many of them would suffer. I speak from experience when I say that both Liverpool and Manchester city centres could look like battle zones in the early hours of a Saturday or Sunday morning. I had nothing but contempt for drunks then and I have nothing but contempt for drunks now.

That morning I went down to the front of the hotel to speak to Boyd and Shaun, who were on the front doors. Suddenly Boyd shot forward, and broke into a run. Now sudden accelerated action by Boyd was unusual to say the least, but having complete faith in him it occurred to me that if he was moving at that speed the rest of us should be too! Both Shaun and I ran after him, and I was a bit perplexed when he continued to run down steep steps not far away. I couldn't imagine what would take him away from the hotel at such a pace, but at the bottom of the steps I saw the reason for his sprint. A young man lay comatose at the foot of a high wall next to the steps. The wall must have been at least fourteen feet high, and I didn't doubt that he had serious injuries. I yelled to Shaun to ring for an ambulance, and knelt down to check the man's breathing. It was shallow but not laboured. Although he was lying on his back, one of his feet was lying at a strange angle; it looked as if he'd damaged his hip or pelvis. Because of this we didn't try to move him. Boyd took off his coat and gently placed it over the unconscious form, and as we waited for the paramedics to arrive I asked Boyd what had happened.

'He was standing by the market, just looking about him, when all of a sudden he started to run, then just leapt over the wall for no apparent reason. It was weird the way he did it. Maybe he didn't know there was a great big drop on the other side. Maybe he did, and he'd had an argument with his girlfriend. Don't know. But it was the suddenness of his movement that caught my eye. It wasn't a natural movement, if you know what I mean.'

We were interrupted by the arrival of the paramedics. The casualty had gained consciousness by this time, and wanted to get to his feet. Despite their every effort by the paramedics to keep him lying down while they examined him, he managed to get up, swaying slightly. I couldn't hear what the medics said to him, and I couldn't hear everything he said to them, but it was obvious he didn't want help. He said he wasn't in any pain, and he didn't even appear to be drunk. He just wanted to be on his way. In the end he signed a disclaimer from the paramedics showing he didn't want any medical treatment, and with a barely discernible limp he walked off.

The paramedics watched him go. 'I can't believe that guy just got up and walked away,' I said.

'Doesn't matter,' came the reply. 'We'll be picking him up later anyway.'

'What do you mean?'

'Did you see the position of his knee and foot?' one of the paramedics asked. 'I think he's broken his pelvis. He'll walk so far, then just collapse; only that time he won't get up again. I've seen it before. The guy's got a life-threatening injury, and he doesn't even know it.'

A fall that could have had extremely serious results took place while the England football team was staying at my favourite hotel. We always provided a full security presence whenever the team arrived at or departed from the hotel, and on this occasion I had been waiting on the ground floor at the bottom of the main staircase, watching for the team to appear two floors up. Just before they came into sight a group of people moved across to the top of the mezzanine stairs and began to descend. I was about to go and ask them to wait for the team to make their way down, when I recognised them as the group accompanying the little girl behind a major charity appeal. I presumed that the child had been in the hotel to meet her football hero, who was in the team.

As the group was well known to the England team, and certainly no threat, I stopped, and was just going to move back towards the centre of reception when something made me look back. One of the men in the party was pulling the little girl's oxygen cylinder, and one of the ladies was carrying the child, connected as always to her cylinder. She stopped at the top of the stairs and placed the little girl on her shoulders before starting to move down the stairs. Thinking this wasn't a good idea for any child, particularly not one connected to an oxygen cylinder, I started back to see if they needed help, or, better still, if I could persuade them to use the lifts. I put my foot on the bottom step, and dropped my gaze to make sure I didn't fall over it (something that happened regularly!), when I heard a loud bang and automatically looked up again towards the group. By this time they were close to the middle section of the stairs, and all I could focus on was the slow but heart-stopping fall of the woman carrying the little girl. I don't know why accidents sometimes appear to occur slowly, but I know from numerous falls from horses that they do. Although I was only a few feet from them I knew there was nothing I could do to reach them in time. With a crash the lady carrying the child ended up in the middle of the flight of stairs, her head facing downwards, with the little girl on top of her. The child was obviously in pain and crying that her leg hurt her, so I asked both of them to keep still so I could discover if there'd been any injuries. As I moved towards the little girl to see if she was still connected to her oxygen supply, a man wearing an England shirt suddenly appeared at my shoulder, and he and another man and woman gently lifted the child off the fallen woman. I recognised the man as a doctor with the England team, and was relieved that they were going to receive instant medical attention. The lady sat up slowly, her main concern being for the child. She kept repeating, 'I had her on my shoulders,' as if trying to convince herself that this had been safe and secure. Apart from the doctor, the girl seemed to be the calmest person present. She stopped crying, and quietly told her mother that she wasn't connected to her oxygen tank. It must have been a terrifying experience for her. Despite several suggestions that she should be taken to hospital for a check-up the party declined, presumably happy with the team doctor's assessment that there were no serious injuries.

It wouldn't be my last experience with the little girl and her entourage, and I never changed my opinion that she was an incredibly brave little girl. I also never changed my opinion that she was a very brave girl surrounded by too many people, a number of whom appeared to be short of the little grey cells.

***

Of course it wasn't always guests who suffered accidents or injuries. Staff accidents, particularly slips, trips and falls, were quite a regular occurrence. However, accidents to guests which were caused by staff were luckily quite rare. An exception to this took place in a Liverpool hotel, when a member of the sales team caused chaos one night as she left work by accidentally running over a guest as he was coming into the hotel! Luckily the injuries weren't fatal. Just to make sure she'd impressed everyone with this action, she more or less repeated the scenario the following night, by running over a different guest in exactly the same spot at exactly the same time. Luckily for this second guest it was only his foot that was injured. I'm still not sure how she managed it.

## CHAPTER FOURTEEN
# FOOTBALL, FOOTBALLERS AND SPORTS EVENTS

I've never been a great fan of football or footballers, but throughout my career in hotels it seemed my lot to look after the security of many of them. The end result was there weren't many footballers I didn't meet, whether I wanted to or not. By and large most behaved themselves. Some were arrogant, some were rude and some were extremely pleasant – just like any cross-section of guests, I suppose. The same could be said for their managers!

Despite those who set out to try to slur his character from time to time, David Beckham was one of the nicest players I met. He was extremely pleasant to everyone, and despite his fame I never heard or saw him put a foot wrong. I found Victoria Beckham equally pleasant.

We dealt with the England team on many occasions. Generally they were no trouble, but the members of the media who followed them were a complete pain. Genuine autograph hunters were on the whole reasonably well behaved, and I could understand their interest in getting pictures or autographs of their heroes. But freelance autograph hunters and paparazzi, whose only interest was to sell pictures and stories, were another thing. It was a twenty-four-hour operation to keep them off hotel property. I never ceased to take great pleasure in removing them from the hotel, or moving them off the car park, where they'd try to set up camp like big game hunters. I suppose that's more or less what they were, and it's more polite to call them hunters rather than the names I usually called them.

We also had dealings with Chelsea, Arsenal, Manchester United, Real Madrid, AC Milan, Portsmouth, Newcastle and probably a dozen more. As far as I was concerned, they were all just another VIP group requiring the usual security protection.

I suppose the individual members of the clubs proved more interesting. I once set fire to my finger while looking after the privacy of the Beckhams and a few other England players and their wives in the lounge of a Manchester hotel! We obviously did our best to keep players and the general public apart, but if the players wanted to spend time in the lounge it was very difficult to keep other guests away from them without major upset. In fairness I took the attitude that if the players wanted to sit in the lounge, and not on their security-controlled floors, then they were fair game for people who wanted to ask for autographs or have photographs taken with them. If their managers were happy for them to have down-time, and occasionally down-time with their wives while they were staying in the hotel, who was I to criticise? But it must be hard to be a football fan, and go for a drink one night in the lounge of your hotel, only to find the England Football Squad sitting a few feet from you; then to top it all, hotel security stopped you from approaching or taking photographs. On the other hand, I didn't want to be on duty when some nutter took a potshot at one of England's leading players. Generally we managed to persuade guests to respect the players' space, leave them alone and admire them from a distance. On the night I set fire to my finger, we had two young women who were desperate to get to David Beckham, who was sitting in the lounge with his wife. Both girls were registered guests (whenever major football teams, players, bands or top celebrities booked into the hotel young fans also booked in), so it was difficult to stop them walking past their idol, or trying to photograph him when they walked past to the toilets. Anyway, quite cleverly, the girls set up a diversion to get us away from the players, using the candle on their table to set fire to some paper. I moved quickly to put it out, radioing Bill as I did so to cover the Beckhams. We stopped the girls from getting to them, but when I went to douse the small flames, I inadvertently spilt burning wax from the candle onto my right index finger, where it continued to burn, making me look like a walking birthday cake until I got to the bar sink to extinguish it. I still have the scar.

I once stopped a fan from asking Ronaldo for an autograph while he was enjoying a quiet drink with a friend. In fairness to the player, he had been quite happy to sign and to pose for photographs. But the policy of the hotel was that we didn't let other guests bother VIPs, so it was my job to stop this from happening (or face an inquisition from the general manager the following day). When I interrupted, Ronaldo said it didn't matter and he didn't mind doing it. I explained about hotel policy, and that I didn't want him bothered all night by a constant stream of people disturbing his evening. He must have thought I sounded like his mother, because he laughed, apologised to the disappointed fan (who wasn't a guest, so I threw him out!), and from then on he called me 'Mamma' when he saw me, sometimes backing this up with a clip round the back of my head. Nice!

Sometimes the problems weren't directly with the players themselves but with what they did without thinking. Whenever we had a leading football player staying at the hotel, he usually arrived via the loading bay at the back. This meant a safer and more controlled entry if fans or the paparazzi were camped at the front. One morning after training he returned, drove his vehicle into the loading bay, then started to change out of his football kit into other clothing. Bill and I had been in the bay, and had brought the shutter down to ensure his safety. When it was obvious that he was about to change before being escorted to his room, we split to cover the other entrances, ensuring that no-one could get through to him. Once he'd changed, he came towards the lifts, and as usual Bill escorted him up to his floor.

Probably twenty minutes later there was a knock at my office door, and one of the housekeeping staff was standing there with an inane grin on her face. 'Is it true you-know-who got his kit off in the loading bay? Did you watch him?' Now I'm old enough to be the guy's grandmother, and I can only repeat that I'm not a fan of football or footballers, so I was quite taken aback by the question. But it got me thinking. Rumours of the lad 'getting his kit off' would soon be all over the hotel. At that time we had an old CCTV tape system, so I played it back – and sure enough the cameras had caught him going from one set of clothing to another. I knew it wouldn't take someone long to work out that by getting hold of a duty manager's key they could access the security room, and it certainly wouldn't be complicated to find the appropriate tape because they were all in date order! I wondered briefly how much a CCTV recording of this particular player stripping would fetch, decided it wouldn't be too long before someone tried to find out, so ejected the tape and destroyed it. You owe me!

Some of the antics players got up to were more serious and would have got them into trouble with their wives, never mind their managers. One such player, and I'm not naming names, was always arrogant and, in my mind, incredibly stupid. I formed this conclusion after watching his antics in the hotel, which included kicking a cardboard box around the reception area while recovering from a broken bone in his foot and wearing flip-flops. Hmm, and he missed major tournaments why ...?!

I remember once returning to the hotel one morning after a weekend off, and checking my emails from team members who'd been on shift that weekend. I was amazed to read one of them. It was from one of the night security officers informing me that he'd seen two England players going into the ladies' toilets with two women to have sex. I duly played back the tape that covered the toilets that night, and sure enough two well-known England players went into the ladies' toilets, but whether or not they had sex was left to the imagination: there were no cameras in the toilets. As far as I was concerned, my role, and that of my security team, was to ensure the safety of guests, and whether they were famous or not their moral or sexual exploits were of no interest to me, as long as they didn't appear in the press or get leaked to the paparazzi, thereby giving the hotel a bad reputation.

However, I knew from experience that this was exactly the sort of story that the press loved. It would also have caused major problems between the two men and their wives or fiancées. But I was mainly annoyed that a member of my team had reported a fact (yes, two footballers did go into the toilets with two girls), then followed it with a supposition (they had sex) and had used the internal email system to relay this information to me. Not the safest way to do it: that's how leaks, gossip and scandal occur. He got an earful from me the next time he was on duty, and a reminder of correct reporting procedures. I also had questions from several staff members during the day as to the truth about the episode, so I assumed I wasn't the only one he'd reported the incident to. And that really was unacceptable. Hotel gossip spreads faster than a bush fire, and hotel moles selling stories to papers can make a lot of money. Just to be on the safe side, I checked the tape one more time, then destroyed it. My team member's attitude to 'stars' in general meant he left shortly afterwards anyway. There's nothing worse than a security officer going all dewy-eyed around the rich and famous.

On one occasion we had an incident in a hotel when AC Milan were staying with us. Their team doctor at the time had allegedly indecently exposed himself to a masseuse worker in the spa. Because of this he was arrested just hours before the kick-off at Old Trafford against Manchester United. The whole incident threw a dark mood over the hotel (it didn't go down too well with AC Milan either). Eventually the young lady dropped the case for personal reasons, but not before the paparazzi spent days camped outside the hotel, trying to sneak in and speak to staff, or stop them as they left the hotel. They truly were muckrakers.

While I worked in a well-known Manchester hotel it hosted an 'after match event' called Soccer Aid. This was part of a major charity event like no other (initiated, I believe, by Robbie Williams and Jonathan Wilkes), which raised millions of pounds in aid of UNICEF UK. The event centred on a football match between two teams comprising celebrities and World Cup legends, one representing England and the other the Rest of the World. The England squad consisted of Robbie Williams (captain), David Gray, Jamie Theakston, Bradley Walsh, Jonathan Wilkes, Ben Shephard, Ronnie O'Sullivan, Damian Lewis, Angus Deayton and Dean Lenno Kelley, with football legends David Seaman, Tony Adams, Paul Gascoigne, Jamie Redknapp, Les Ferdinand, John Barnes, Bryan Robson and Graeme Le Saux. The Rest of the World squad consisted of celebrities Gordon Ramsay (captain), David Campese, Patrick Kielty, Gareth Thomas, Ben Johnson, Sergei Fedorov, Brian McFadden, Alastair Campbell, Craig Doyle, Alessandro Nivola, Michael Greco, and football legends Gianfranco Zola, Marcel Desailly, David Ginola, Dunga, Lothar Matthaus, Peter Schmeichel, Diego Maradona, with Ruud Gullit and Gustavo Poyet as players and managers. The VIP list was endless, with the event taking over the whole hotel. The event organisers, Endemol, were a global leader in entertainment programming, and I believe the largest television and digital production company in the world. That more or less summed up the size and scale of the event.

Bill and I had worked a twenty-hour shift during the event, being there for the hotel close-down the previous night, the event itself, and eventually helping the last drunken stragglers to bed or out of the front doors the following morning. My final memory of the event was of standing in the absolute peace and quiet of the reception area the following morning, mulling over the evening's incidents and wondering just how many reports I had to write, when the silence was broken by the car park buzzer. I looked across to the concierge desk, where the communication system between the hotel and exit barrier was housed. One of the young concierge lads who'd just come on duty was about to answer it, and I watched his hand move towards the barrier release button. The only time the buzzer sounded was if someone wanted to be let out without paying, or if there was a problem with the barrier. I knew the latter wasn't true.

'No, stop! Don't open the barrier. What's the problem?' I shouted across.

'Someone wants to be let out,' he replied, his hand poised over the release key.

My patience that night had been tried way beyond what could have been expected of a mere mortal, and although I knew I was still awake, this was only because I was upright and not lying on the ground. I didn't think my feet or body would move again, ever. So, seeing the fresh face of a member of staff, who luckily had been able to sleep in a bed the previous night, about to perform a task because he was too lazy to check it was OK to let the car out ... I guess it's fair to say that I snapped at the poor lad.

'Don't open that barrier. There's a few million pounds' worth of vehicles parked there. Who is it?'

'Don't know', came back the startled reply.

'Well if you don't bloody know, don't bloody well open the barrier, you idiot.'

The buzzer sounded again, only longer and more impatiently.

'Go and have a look through the window, and see if you know who they are,' I yelled. He was considerably closer than I was, and I could just imagine the follow-up if a vehicle was stolen from the car park because someone couldn't be bothered to check that the driver was the lawful owner.

The lad had only moved a few paces when the front doors were flung open (not easy, as they were heavy glass), and a faded but well-known footballer stood swaying in the doorway.

'That's my fucking father. Let him out.'

Now at any other time I'd have made an assessment of this request based on the individual VIP guest, the driver of the vehicle, the loss of revenue by not charging for parking, the level of aggression, threat and disruption to other guests, as well as several other factors that each individual demand for free parking brought with it. But this morning I'd just about had enough of footballers, event guests, invited guests, non-invited guests, their relations and their appalling bad manners. I was a woman on the edge. This guy meant nothing to me, and nor did his father. I was suddenly tired of dealing with spoilt footballers and boring celebrities, who despite the fact that they were probably millionaires in their own right, had in some cases wandered around the hotel lifting left-over wine bottles to their mouths in an attempt to drink the last tiny drop of alcohol because it was free. I'd despised those drunken guests who'd been abusive, vomited on pristine carpets, dropped glasses throughout the hotel because they were too drunk to hold them, and who had treated staff like slaves while being treated as gods themselves. I was fed up with hearing the words 'Do you know who I am? Of course he can come into the hotel' and 'Of course he can come in; he's with me.' I had despised the so-called VIPs, like the well-known journalist, broadcaster, political aide and acknowledged 'spin doctor' who'd punched a member of my security team because he refused to allow him to bring someone into the party who wasn't on the official list and wasn't wearing the appropriate security band. My guy had only been carrying out the written instructions of the organisers: we didn't make up the rules and regulations, we merely upheld them. Because he was so drunk, the individual didn't even realise that the assault took place in front of a uniformed police officer. Had I been there at the time, I would certainly have followed the policeman's advice to have him arrested for assault. But there you are: I'd been two floors up, dealing with a couple of footballers who believed they could also take guests wherever they wanted, despite the organisers' insistence that coloured security wrist bands restricted access for some guests. The unlucky security officer had decided that because of his assailant's status it wouldn't be good for either the hotel or his attacker to be arrested on the steps of the hotel, particularly with an army of photographers camped outside. Good for him, a truly noble gesture – which I hasten to add went without any thanks or apologies either from the hotel or the well-known individual. I only found out about the incident later, and at the request of the security officer I didn't pursue it. I should have done. I was wrong.

So, after handling a night of people I despised and had little but contempt for, the footballer and his father suddenly seemed to typify all the stupid, drunken, abusive, aggressive and sometimes violent so-called VIPs of the previous night, and I found myself saying, 'Has he paid for his parking, Mr ...?

I'll leave his reply to your imagination. And, no, I wouldn't have let him out without paying. Unfortunately the concierge lad was closer to the release button than I was.

I think one of the most bizarre moments of the whole event had been the arrival of Maradona, and his entrance up the main staircase of the hotel. What an entrance it was too! Word spread like wildfire that he was making his way up the two-floor stairway to the main event, and literally hundreds of people ran to any part of the stairs that might offer a view of the man. Slowly a chant that had been used during his World Cup days started to reverberate from ground to second floor. There seemed to be so many people that I wondered whether any of them had gained access via fire doors without me knowing, and that we were breaking fire regulations by having too many people in the building. The chant grew louder and louder, and because of its uniformity and volume I actually felt the stairs shuddering. Pictures on the first-floor gallery vibrated on the walls. It was surreal. Yet still they chanted, '... Donna, wo oh oh oh', over and over again at the top of their voices. Bill joined me on the second floor to look down at Maradona's slow and deliberate progress up the stairs, a dark coat casually hanging from his shoulders. He had presence, I'll give him that.

'So what's this all about?' I asked.

'No idea,' came Bill's reply. 'Suppose he's some sort of hero to them,' he added without any enthusiasm.

I thought about this for a few moments, the chanting banging in my head. 'So, have I got this wrong then? Is this the same guy who supposedly cheated us out of the World Cup by using his hand to knock the ball into the net?'

'Yep.'

'But they all think he's a hero, not a cheat?'

'Yep.'

'How does that work?'

'No idea,' repeated Bill with the same lack of interest, and he wandered off to check another part of the hotel. I guess I wasn't the only one with no interest in football or footballers!

After Maradona's visit to the hotel, the security team (which managed all lost property) ended up with his dinner jacket. Despite all our efforts to try and return it, no-one ever bothered to reply to my emails or telephone calls, so for a long time it hung in our office, waiting for someone to either claim it or tell us where to return it to. It never happened. Eventually, months later and just before I left the hotel, Bill and I spent an evening sorting lost property into separate piles: items that were waiting to be claimed by owners who knew they were there but never turned up to collect them; those of value that we hoped someone would claim eventually; and those that were possibly of value and had been in our possession for months, but it was doubtful anyone would claim.

Maradona's jacket went into the first heap, and in the end it was placed with a lot of other items in one of the hotel's compactors and destroyed. It seemed a terrible waste, but if no-one wanted it I certainly didn't want it cluttering up my office any more. As the compactor slowly ground everything into unrecognisable mush, Bill gave a theatrical sigh. 'Do you know how much that would have fetched on the internet? Why are we so honest?' It wasn't a question that required an answer, nor did he expect one, so I just laughed. It wasn't that we minded being honest; we just got sick of people leaving their property behind when they left the hotel.

The following year the UFC (Ultimate Fighting Championship) came to the Manchester Evening News Arena (MENA), and their management team and several of the fighters stayed at the hotel. It caused quite a sensation at the time, with members of our management team convinced that the hotel would be reduced to a pile of bricks and rubble before their stay was out. They were, in fact, all incredibly well behaved, and apart from having a few fighters return to the hotel with faces that looked as if they'd taken on King Kong and lost, their stay went peacefully. Mind you, having seen some of the fighters it was obvious they didn't have anything to prove, and it would have taken an incredibly stupid person to upset them.

During their stay we had a selection of other celebrities as guests, including a famous martial artist who had a string of movies to his credit. As he mixed with the UFC guys I presumed he knew one or two of them, and that he'd come over to support one of them in particular. I only had a brief encounter with him, and this was when a well-known football team was leaving in a coach from the front of the hotel. I was standing by the door to the coach as usual, to ensure that photographers didn't attempt to board it, or get photographs they weren't entitled to take, when I realised that someone who definitely wasn't a footballer was striding towards me with the intention of getting aboard. As normal I moved to block his entrance, and said, as I always did, 'I'm sorry, sir, this is a private coach.' The guy was merely inches from me, and had only stopped because to continue would have meant physically moving me out of the way. I could see surprise in his eyes: someone had actually stopped him from doing what he wanted! He spoke to me, but I couldn't catch what he said, and then he gesticulated that he wanted to board the coach, making a slight move forward. I didn't move, and repeated that the coach was a private one. It was then that I recognised him as the actor, and for a split second I wondered how I'd fare against one of his legendary kicks, and whether I could grab a delicate part of his body before his foot connected with my head. I was just losing this imaginary battle when a couple of the footballers recognised him and invited him onto the coach. I paused just long enough for their manager to agree before stepping aside. Later that day Bill and I had been laughing about this stand-off when another member of staff joined us, unaware of what we were talking about. 'Did you see that karate actor in reception?' I was just about to reply that I'd been seeing him on and off all day and still wasn't impressed, when he continued, 'He was crying like a baby because his mate lost his fight.'

Bill started to chuckle. 'That's probably your fault for bullying him earlier in the day! Bet he writes and complains about your appalling behaviour.'

I must admit I haven't watched one of his films since; he kind of lost his shine in my eyes after that.

During my time in hotels I met several professional fighters. If I had any favourites, they were probably two boxers local to the North-West. I found both of them professional and courteous, not just to their fans but also to the hotel staff who looked after them. Unfortunately I probably got off to a bad start with the family of one of the boxers when I first met them. On the night in question this young lad was staying at the hotel, which was closed to everyone but residents. As normal Bill and I were on the front doors listening to the usual, 'Of course we can come in. Do you know who I am?' We were aware that the lad would be returning straight after his fight, and had been looking out for him. Many of his fans had also been looking out for his return, and we'd turned away at least a dozen 'sisters', 'brothers', 'aunts', 'uncles' and 'cousins'. It had been an extremely long day, and in truth both Bill and I had been on duty too long, and had had enough of people who hoped they were clever enough to bully us into allowing them in. But there was no-one to replace us: it was us or no security cover at all. Typical hotels really.

At that time in the early hours, when your feet are killing you because you've been on them for over twelve hours, when bed appears a million miles off and people seem to be the lowest form of life, a group of about five men and women had approached us. We went through the usual 'Good evening, Sir, Madam. Are you staying in the hotel tonight? May I see your resident's card?'. One of the men, who like everyone else I'd dealt with that night appeared to have had too much to drink, went through the thoroughly boring routine of 'We're not staying tonight, but we're with the boxer's party' (all said in a strong South Wales accent). I'd heard this one time too many, and I said without thinking, 'Yes, sir, and so are a hundred other people who've tried to get into the hotel tonight.' The conversation went downhill from there; my fault for handling it incorrectly at the outset.

'No, seriously, I'm his uncle, see, and this is his sister, and these are his cousins like.'

'And I believe you,' I'd replied, wincing at the strong accent, 'but unfortunately we have several large groups in the hotel tonight, and equally unfortunately only residents will be allowed in the hotel.'

'Yes, but we're 'ere to meet him like.'

'You'll be disappointed, then. I'm afraid you won't be meeting him in the hotel.'

'No, you 'ave to let us in, see, 'cause we're part of 'is family, like, and we told him we'd meet him here.'

For some reason the conversation had begun to wind me up. Too many people had spun this yarn in one night I suppose.

'I don't have to let you in at all. I don't have to let anyone in who isn't a resident, and as you must be the fiftieth person this evening who's told me they're an uncle or brother or cousin or sister to – I mentioned the boxer's name – I don't even have to believe you're telling me the truth.'

'Oh, right, well, I am 'is uncle, see,' and he turned to the rest of the open-mouthed group. 'Aren't I?'

'Oh yes, he is, you know. We're 'is cousins, and she's 'is sister.'

By this time they seemed to me as if they were from the valley of the damned, and even though they'd all obviously been drinking, I knew I wasn't handling them in a particularly professional way. The trouble was, I really didn't care.

'Right. I've got a good idea which should work for all of us. You stay there on the steps, and when he returns and confirms you're all part of his family I'll be happy to let you into the hotel, even though my general manager will ask me in the morning why I couldn't follow a simple rule of 'No resident card, no entry.' How does that seem to you?'

'Oh that's fine, see, 'cause I'm his uncle, and these are 'is cousins, see, and his sister, and we made arrangements to meet him in the hotel after 'is fight, so if you just let us in, we can talk to 'im, see?'

The only thing I'd seen was a red mist slowly descending, and I was getting fed up with the word 'see'.

'Right, let's get this straight. You're not coming in now, you're not coming in later, and if you don't stop blocking the steps and the passage of legitimate residents into this hotel, you're not coming in when your nephew comes back either – even if he really is your nephew.'

'Oh, that's not right. I'm his uncle. What do you think I am, some kind of nuisance who just wants to get a late night drink in a swanky hotel?'

'What I think,' I answered, knowing I was in danger of losing it completely and forgetting professionalism and civility altogether, 'is irrelevant. Until your supposed nephew returns to the hotel none of your party's going into the hotel, and as far as I'm concerned that's the end of it.'

I could feel Bill's presence. We'd worked together for so long that I knew he would realise I was about to develop what's commonly known as tunnel vision, and that I was about to do or say something I'd very much regret. But the guy would not be silenced.

'Go on,' he started again, upset that I was doubting his word. 'Go on, tell me what you think I am.'

It was too much, and I was too tired. Even before I spoke I knew I was about to do something I'd not done in the ten years I'd been working in hotels. 'What do I think? Let me tell you what I think.' And then I did.

Bill grabbed the collar of my jacket, and instead of facing the stunned group, I found myself facing the opposite direction, looking back into the reception area of the hotel. Bill's hand firmly pushed me towards the desk. 'Go get a coffee,' he hissed. 'I really can't believe you said that.'

Neither could I, but I guess everyone has their breaking point. It was the first and last time I was ever so rude to a guest in a hotel (unless they really deserved it), and I wasn't proud of myself.

I have to be honest too. When the boxer returned to the hotel after his fight, guess what: they really were his uncle, sister and cousins!

## CHAPTER FIFTEEN

# VIP AND CELEBRITY VISITS

I f I didn't like footballers it was equally true to say that there weren't many celebrities I liked either – although there were a few exceptions. Now I don't have idols, and if I did they would belong anywhere but in the celebrity field, but I was (and still am) a long-time fan of Meatloaf! I also found Robbie Williams an incredibly nice person to work with (as did all his staff), and as I've said Kylie Minogue was an extremely pleasant person to look after.

Most celebrity visits went the same way. I would get word from the sales manager that a band, group or A-lister planned to stay in the hotel on a certain day, and I'd contact their close protection operative (CPO) to make sure they had all the information about the hotel they needed. I would also ensure their team or teams were aware of emergency procedures, fire and evacuation plans, escape routes and so on.

If the VIPs were government officials, members of the royal family or foreign dignitaries, their people usually contacted me directly before the sales team knew anything about it. I'd then liaise with their close protection teams, Special Branch, the local police force and sometimes foreign embassies to ensure that all went well with their visit. I felt a close affinity with these teams, because I knew what it was like to look after someone who was genuinely threatened. I also knew from personal experience that all too often those who were forgotten, seldom even thought about and rarely fed or watered, were their own CPOs! During these visits I always made sure that if a hot meal couldn't be prepared for them because of their tight schedule, at least platters of sandwiches and flasks of coffee were on hand. Part of me always missed the buzz of the job, even though I knew the period in which you can work as a CPO is short; and I was well past that period. Still, it was always good to work with professional people.

Needless to say, there were many so-called CPOs who wouldn't have known how to look after a cardboard cut-out, never mind a high-risk principal with a genuine death threat against them. As much as possible I tried to ignore these armchair warriors: they were usually bad news, flapped like headless chickens and generally created a dramatic environment when there should have been peace and tranquillity.

Inevitably, of course, having guests stay with us who genuinely needed protection against serious harm, or even assassination, brought with them specific problems, concerns, risks and even humour.

A memory is already there.


*Manchester. The prime minister and his wife are due in about an hour's time: their suite, shining and spotless, is awaiting their arrival. I'm with the police dog handlers and their two detection dogs while they check the last floor for any explosive devices. We're running a bit late, but there is now only the main suite to check. The executive housekeeper comes in just before the dogs enter the luxury rooms. As she's going through every last detail the dog team arrives, and she hurries to finish. Ten minutes later I tell her she has to leave; we've run out of time. A consummate professional, she knows all this: she's been through it as many times as I have. As she leaves she automatically runs her hand over the back of the couch, smoothing out any imaginary creases; the suite is so clean it gleams. I unlock all doors and riser cupboards, then step back to let the* police and their dogs do their job. The younger of the two dogs, a springer spaniel, jumps on the bed to sniff around the pillows, then leaps across onto a comfy chair nearby. I'm glad the housekeeper isn't present, this could have brought on a fit of the vapours. The dog's handler gesticulates to the dog to move on to another area; I'm sure he is totally unmoved by the deep prints and dog hair on the previously pristine quilt cover. Efficient and focused, they move from room to room within the suite. The bedroom is clear, the lounge is clear, the bathrooms are clear. Then they move into the kitchen. The spaniel instantly sits down in front of a large round waterpipe in the corner and looks back at his handler. It's called 'presenting', and means the dog has detected some sort of explosive.

The police officer asks for the second dog to be brought in, removing his now excitable partner from the kitchen. When this dog enters the kitchen it also sits and wags its tail at the pipe.

The police now want to gain access to the ceiling of the kitchen close to the pipe. Steps are sent for, and several sections of the false ceiling are removed. Dust from the exposed ceiling drifts down onto the floor, and large clumps of damaged ceiling tiles fall onto the gleaming kitchen counters. Torches flash above us, and as other police officers come in their shoes transfer dust and dirt from the kitchen to the well-hoovered carpet of the lounge. There is a lot of banging, pulling and pushing of the pipe. I can hear things rattling down the inside of it, but have total faith in the police that they know what they are doing. Ten minutes later the head of the team climbs back down the step ladder. His face and hair are white with dust, his hands are grimy, but he has a smile on his face. He asks for the dogs to be brought back individually. When they return, neither dog shows interest in the kitchen or the pipe.

'Nail guns' he says. 'The dogs pick up on the small explosive charge they use. Incredible, really. When they build hotels bits of the charge can get stuck in roofs, pipes and so on: you just have to clear all the bits away. The dogs are happy then, and if the dogs are happy, I'm happy. Thought we were going to have to pull the kitchen apart for a few moments!'

*I look around me at what had once been a clean and orderly kitchen. Dusty footprints form a well-defined path from the kitchen to the front doors of the suite. As I walk past the bedroom I see that at least one of the dogs has checked out the bed again. I look at my watch, then radio the housekeeper to come to the suite with an army of her staff. She arrives a few minutes later, purple in the face. 'Do you know one of those dogs has peed against the doors of the guest lift ...' she starts. Then there's silence as her eyes take in the state of the VIP suite. 'Wonderful animals those dogs,' I say as I pass her. 'I'll just go and get maintenance to put the kitchen ceiling back!'*

*I don't know how she did it (although the PM being late certainly helped), but when his party arrived the suite was spotlessly clean again.*

Queen Rania of Jordan was probably one of the most beautiful women I've ever seen. I was working in a London hotel when she visited as a guest speaker at a conference held at the hotel, and although I had no grounds at all to believe her visit would be anything other than peaceful, she was nonetheless royalty, and normal security procedures for a royal visit were put in place.

Usually before a royal visit the police would carry out a full search and, similar to a visit by a prime minister, use detection dogs to check for any explosive devices. For some reason this hadn't happened this time, so a couple of hours before her arrival, despite lacking the nose of a cocker spaniel, I routinely checked everywhere she was likely to walk, sit or speak, just to see if anything looked out of place. I even checked the female toilets on the fifth floor where, immediately after her arrival, she was to be escorted to a VIP lounge set aside for her. I had been asked by the head of her security team to show them the route she would take, and also to escort the queen, her bodyguards and entourage to and from the fifth floor, and down the labyrinth of stairs and corridors to the conference on the first floor. It was a very easy hotel to get lost in. When she arrived she was surrounded by ceremony and bodyguards, who immediately wanted her whisked off to the fifth floor. I led her procession up, then stood slightly apart from the formal line of dignitaries, automatically checking the people around me while she went into the VIP lounge. Nothing seemed out of the ordinary; there was no reason why it should be. I wasn't aware of any threat against her, but possibly a thousand people were waiting in the conference centre four floors below, all eager to hear her speak. I had no doubt that some would raise both political and feminist issues – and that not all would agree with her point of view.

The doors of the VIP lounge opened and the queen's party started to trickle out. I made one last visual check, and everything still seemed normal. As I moved towards the stairwell door, ready to guide the party down, the group suddenly stopped. I realised the queen was carrying a voice mike and wire in her hand, and watched as she slipped into the ladies' toilets, presumably to thread the mike beneath her blouse and out onto her collar. I stood back and watched the line form again. I waited, and her entourage and line of hopeful handshakers waited. We waited an unusually long time, but she still showed no sign of coming out. Concerned, I realised she could have threaded a dozen mikes through her clothes by now. It was obvious I wasn't the only one getting concerned. People around me had become restless; her bodyguards shifted nervously outside the toilet door; her hosts surreptitiously glanced at watches. I considered offering to go in and check that she was OK, but bulging armpits and twitchy fingers from the big guys looking after her dissuaded me.

I continued to wait at the very end of the line, hoping for her return and for the party to turn round and follow me down the stairs. I was probably as far as I could be from the queen. Then, with a sudden flash of insight that made my stomach churn, I realised why she hadn't come out. She was lost in a one-way system! Not only that, it was a one-way system with inadequate signage. On the far side of the toilets there were exit doors conveniently hidden by four rows of cubicles and two white tiled walls. The old exit signs had fallen off months ago and hadn't been replaced. It wouldn't be the first time we had lost startled and confused guests in those toilets, but never a queen! It was like a maze in there if you didn't know your way through them. Looking around, I realised that no-one else had considered this predicament. Very slowly, taking particular care not to upset the suited guys talking into their sleeves, I edged my way along the line to the conference and banqueting manager somewhere near the front of the queue.

'She's been in there quite a long time,' I whispered.

'I know,' he hissed back.

I considered my timing before dropping the bombshell. 'Do you think she knows how to get out?'

He turned his head sharply towards me with a scathing comment ready, and then the penny dropped. His face went through a few thousand expressions as the colour drained from it. 'Oh God', he said, and I saw him visualising the next day's headlines: 'Hotel Locks Queen in Toilets.' He groaned loud enough to attract the attention of her close protection team.

'I suppose I could go in,' I whispered. We both looked across at her bodyguards. They looked nervous, twitchy and completely without humour. 'Not a good idea,' I acknowledged. 'She must have a lady in waiting somewhere.'

He nodded, and trying not to look conspicuous started to sidle up the line to the conference organiser. Again there was a quick whisper and the dropping of heads, trying to hold a conversation that was not meant for others to overhear. I watched the organiser's head snap to attention and a look of shock flash across his face. Then quietly, without wishing to cause alarm, he moved ghost-like along the line until he reached the end. A delicate cough, and he had the attention of a smartly dressed woman waiting closest to the toilet doors. Once more the hushed communication, the sharp intake of breath and again the look of shock. I presumed that this was the lady in waiting, because without hesitation, and without getting shot, she immediately sped into the toilets.

Seconds later both queen and lady in waiting re-emerged. Not a word was spoken; not an ounce of accusation was uttered. With a dignity and serenity I could only admire, the royal visitor slowly and calmly walked down the line of waiting people towards me, smiling sweetly to those she passed, her voice mike pinned neatly on her blouse.

Without any further interruption I led the party down the flights of stairs and into the conference hall. A standing ovation met her entrance, from an international multitude wishing to show respect and admiration for the royal guest. I stood to the side and waited. I felt better keeping her in sight; she just might want to visit the toilets again!

Not all VIP visits were coupled with humour of course, but sometimes even a serious incident ended with an amusing anecdote.

Tony Blair was prime minister when he visited Liverpool and the hotel I worked in. By the time he arrived I knew most of the CPOs and police officers who would be present. These ranged from members of Special Branch to uniformed police and senior police officers. It seemed as if half of Liverpool's police force would be in or around the hotel for the visit. However, from my point of view, dealing with a prime minister's visit wasn't complicated; it just involved raising security levels in relation to the threat.

I have never had a great interest in politics and certainly don't have a favourite party. So dealing with politicians was always easy – I took them as I found them, and judged them accordingly. I had met Tony Blair on a couple of occasions, and he always came across as pleasant and professional, and more importantly he took time to speak to all members of staff he met (including security). Minutes before his arrival I met some of his security advance party, and also spoke to the senior police officer in charge, who had based himself at the front of the hotel. Everyone was happy, everyone who should have been in place was in place, and it seemed as if the visit would proceed problem -free and on time. Sure enough, I received a mobile phone call from one of his CPOs to say they were just pulling into the hotel, and with the usual precision a blacked-out Range Rover and two or three black limousines pulled up in front of the doors. Tony Blair stepped into the hotel, and with a wave and 'hello' to everyone headed towards me at the main lifts, where I had the middle lift keyed off ready for him. He shook my hand as he always did, then stepped into the lift with his chief CPO and a couple of his close advisors. They didn't need me to show them where to go; that information had already been relayed to his No. 1 when I'd walked the route with the advance party.

As the lift door closed behind them my role was temporarily over, and I started to walk back to the front doors to check the PM's departure time with his driver. I'd nearly reached the front of the hotel when a member of my security team came rushing over to me, clearly in an agitated state.

'There's been a road accident outside. Guy knocked off his bike!' he shouted breathlessly. 'Has anyone called an ambulance'? I asked. 'Don't know' came the reply. I started to run the last couple of yards to the front doors, asking him to fetch the trauma pack I always kept in my office for major injuries. I saw Steve McGee leave his position at the far door and start running after me. I should have known, I thought, with Steve and me both on duty at the same time something like this was bound to happen!

An extremely high brick wall separated the main entrance to the hotel from the busy road outside, and I could see nothing until I turned the corner of the wall. Two or three cars were slewed across the highway, a woman on the pavement was crying into a mobile phone, and a large pool of blood was spreading across the road from the group bent over something in front of the cars. It didn't look good. As I ran up, I saw two men holding tightly to belts attached to the top of the casualty's leg. I presumed the belts were their own, and I presumed they were trying to restrict an arterial bleed. Blood seemed to have flown freely and without restriction from beneath the man's left leg, and he appeared to be semiconscious. I knew that tourniquets were seen as bad news, and first aid instructors taught that they should only ever be used in a dire emergency. This situation looked like a dire emergency. I asked the two guys if they were first aiders, and they shook their heads. 'No,' one of them replied, 'but his leg was spurting blood. I think he's ruptured an artery. He'll bleed to death if we remove these.'

I agreed with the diagnosis. 'Has anyone sent for an ambulance?', I asked for the second time. One of the men nodded towards the woman on the phone. 'She's talking to them now.'

I knelt down beside the injured man and took hold of his hand. I could feel the stickiness of blood on my knees and shins. Steve knelt down on the other side. We made eye contact, then Steve turned to take hold of the trauma kit as it arrived.

I turned to the casualty. 'Can you hear me?'

There was a flicker of acknowledgement from the grey face.

'My name's Sue. I'm a first aider, and I'm going to stay with you until the paramedics arrive. There's an ambulance on its way. They'll be here soon. You've injured your left leg, but these guys have stopped it bleeding. You're going to be OK. I'm just going to have a look at it to see if there's anything I can do to help.' I realised I'd probably overdosed him with information, but a very slight nod came back.

I quickly checked his body for any other injuries, then moved down to the lower part of his left leg. Blood was still seeping out, but it wasn't flowing as much as it had been. The injury seemed to be at the back of his leg, but as I tried to gently move his leg to get a closer look, the guy screamed in agony. I left it where it was. I could see that at least part of his calf had been ripped away.

'How long has the tourniquet been on?' I asked.

'We've literally just put it on.'

I did a quick mental calculation about ambulance arrival time, time needed to move the leg and cover the wound, and the length of time the blood supply to his lower leg had effectively been cut off. Then added the effects of shock if I caused him any more pain.

'OK, let's leave it on for a bit longer.' I turned to the casualty. 'What's your name?'

He gave it, then started to drift into unconsciousness, which was something I didn't want.

Just then the young lady on the mobile phone came across. She was ashen, and was obviously in shock. I later learned that she was the driver who'd knocked the cyclist off his bike, but I never learned whose fault it was. 'I'm onto the emergency services. They say don't put a tourniquet on his leg.'

'What?' I whispered.

'They say take the tourniquet off. You're not supposed to put one on.'

The two men (I later found out they were lorry drivers who had witnessed the accident) looked a bit startled.

'Don't move that tourniquet,' I said to them. Then I turned to the young lady. 'Give me your phone and let me speak to them.'

I had to stand up to get the phone, and Steve leaned over the casualty to continue reassuring him. As I stood, something tickled the front of my shin, and I looked down to see that blood was running down my leg from where I'd knelt on the floor. Remove the tourniquet; yes, like hell I would. I took the phone off the girl, immediately covering the front of it with blood. She looked as if she was going to say something, then changed her mind. I informed the emergency operator that in my opinion the guy's life would be in jeopardy if the tourniquet was removed, or even loosened, and after a few seconds of heated debate she agreed that it could stay on so long as I loosened it after about ten minutes. I handed the bloody phone back to the young lady, praying feverishly that the paramedics would arrive a lot quicker than that. I hoped my assessment of the tourniquet was correct. What if I was wrong? What if he lost his leg because the tourniquet was left on too long? I wasn't a doctor; I wasn't a paramedic. But I'd looked at the blood loss on the ground, and couldn't think of an alternative to the tight bandage.

Steve had managed to get a dressing under the wound as the casualty moved slightly, but from the look in his eyes he was praying as much as I was for the wonderful sound of an emergency vehicle. I knelt down again beside the man. His eyes were open, his pupils dilated, and his breathing was irregular. 'The ambulance won't be long now,' I tried to reassure him. 'Do you have anyone I could contact to let them know about your accident?'

In a low voice, contorted with pain, the man gave me the name of his daughter and a telephone number for her. I'd just written this down when there was a strange noise to my right, and when I looked up I saw four of the longest horse legs I'd ever seen. I continued upwards, and somewhere miles in the sky a mounted police officer looked down at me.

'You OK?' he asked.

'Yes. An ambulance is on its way,' I replied, not wanting to talk about the injured man in front of him. 'An ambulance will be here soon,' I repeated again to the man on the ground. It seemed to be the only thing I was capable of saying.

'Right, I'll get back then,' said the police officer, and he turned his horse and rode off. I wondered if he'd got off his horse and I'd held it, he would have been able to do more than I had, which at that moment seemed to be nothing at all.

Seconds later I heard the sound of an ambulance, and bent over the casualty to let him know. We made eye contact for a few seconds, and he whispered 'thank you', which I really didn't deserve because I hadn't actually done anything.

I indicated with my head to the two lorry drivers still holding their belts tight on his thigh. 'No problems. Those guys are the ones who really helped you.' After reassuring him that I'd contact his daughter, I stood up to pass the incident to the experts.

There was nothing left for me to do. I remembered our VIP visitor, so left Steve to assist and walked back towards the hotel. I hated people hanging around the scene of an accident when they've got nothing to do except get in the way. Just before I entered the hotel I remembered the blood on my legs, and when I looked down was shocked to see my skirt, legs and shoes all covered in blood. As there was also blood on my hands, I realised I must look as if I'd just murdered someone. Luckily at that moment one of the housekeeping staff arrived, and I got her to open a fire door to let me in. I stripped, showered, then wrapped myself in an enormous fluffy white hotel towel, and waited a very short time for housekeeping to wash and dry practically every stitch of clothing I had. Thanks to them, I was back in the reception area within forty minutes, just in time to shake hands with Tony Blair as he left the hotel!

It was only after he'd gone that one of the Special Branch guys I knew came up to me and started laughing. I asked what was funny.

179

'You caused chaos.' When I asked him what he meant he started laughing again, and said that when I'd run out of the hotel one of the uniformed police officers outside the hotel had thought something was wrong. He'd run after me to find out what it was. The senior police officer on the front door had seen one of his constables running, so he ran after him. Then one of Tony Blair's close protection team stationed in reception saw the senior police officer start to run, so he ran in the same direction! As this guy ran he was joined by another member of the close protection team standing by one of the vehicles, and seeing us run round the wall, they decided that it would be quicker for them to run as fast as they could towards it, leap up and look over the top.

I thought about the height of the wall. 'Did they make it?'

'Did they hell. They both hit the wall three-quarters of the way up, and rebounded off into the bushes.' He was doubled up laughing. 'It was the funniest thing I ever saw.'

Later that day I received a phone call from the police with the best possible news. The casualty would survive, and despite fears that he might lose his leg it now seemed highly probable that he'd keep it. I was really made up. My only regret was that I didn't have contact names or numbers for the two lorry drivers, whose quick reactions had without doubt saved a life. They were real heroes.

A couple of weeks later I received a letter from Merseyside Police apologising for the fact that despite a large police presence around the hotel none of them had actually helped with the road traffic accident. I hadn't thought about it at the time, but looking back I suppose it was odd; equally, though, they all had their allotted roles to play in looking after the prime minister, so I guess they had their hands full.

Apart from Queen Rania, I didn't really have a lot to do with royal visits. But our paths did cross on occasion. I only met Prince William once. He came to a Manchester hotel while the England football team was in residence. I can't remember if he came to train with them or just to meet them during training, but I do remember what a nice guy he was when he returned to the hotel. I'd been holding a lift open for his return: normally I'd have held the lifts for the England players, but obviously William took priority. His protection team had told me that William would return first, go up to a meeting room, then the team would return. As usual it seemed simple enough – but it all went wrong when they all returned together. A couple of the players automatically approached the lift I was holding open, and I had to turn them away, explaining it was being held for someone else. When Prince William arrived shortly afterwards the players gave him a hard time for taking status priority! He took it all in good fun, retorting, 'Sorry, guys, but you'll just have to wait for the next one,' then gave me a beaming smile as he got into the lift.

He was certainly a lot nicer than another royal, who had a tantrum in a London hotel where I worked, and publicly berated his close protection team for doing something minor. I felt like reminding him that they were there to protect his life, and would have willingly stood between him and a bullet if necessary – well, perhaps not willingly! When I spoke to one of his guys later I asked if he was always that bad tempered, and he replied, 'Yes – most of the time!'

On separate occasions I dealt with both Prince and Princess Michael of Kent: both charming people. I had little to do with Princess Michael, who was gracing a book club signing. Prince Michael's visit was a little more eventful. Just as he entered the Liverpool hotel, one of my team decided to radio and ask me to let him know when the VIP was due, as he was dealing with an incident on one of the floors.

As radio silence was normally the requirement of these occasions, and I didn't expect any radio communication, I foolishly still had my radio on – and turned up to full volume! In that solemn moment of silence, with the prince directly in front of me, his voice boomed: 'Sue, it's me. Let me know when that prince bloke comes in, will you? I'm dealing with a right couple of plonkers on the tenth floor.'

Thanks for that! It really helped our careers, and nearly caused a major incident with his close protection teams: the sudden noise of the radio almost produced concealed weapons. Prince Michael, however, never batted an eyelid. He merely smiled as he passed.

I don't recall how many celebrities I dealt with during my career. But I do know that one day out of interest I started to list them. I gave up after filling four pages of a notebook because they'd all begun to merge into a blur of boring similarity. But inevitably some stood out. I've mentioned before that I'm a Meatloaf fan. When I first met the guy, I'd been waiting for several hours past the tour manager's estimated time of arrival for his tour coaches to appear. When they finally arrived it was the early hours of the morning, and although there'd been a fan club reception earlier, a cold wind and heavy rain had driven them all away. There was just me left. The first coach with his band, backing group, lead singer and a few others who no doubt did important things, arrived and more or less fell out of the coach together. I had no idea if they'd had a few drinks along the way or were just so tired that they couldn't stand, but they all had a single question: 'Is the bar still open?' It was, and they all disappeared upstairs towards it. They were extremely nice guys and gals, particularly one of his female singers – who always used to stop and chat before she disappeared into the hotel, which was practically unheard of.

When Meatloaf's coach arrived nobody got off. I was beginning to wonder if I'd missed him or he'd decided to arrive by another form of transport, when he appeared slowly round the coach and stood on the pavement at the foot of the hotel steps. He looked completely and utterly exhausted; there was no other word for it. He swayed slightly and stood looking up the steps as if considering whether his body would make it. Had I thought it appropriate I'd have offered to help, because I really doubted that he was going to make it up unaided. But he dragged himself up the steps, and I acknowledged the guy walking beside him, who I presumed was his tour manager, got a half-smile from Meatloaf, then escorted them to their rooms. From that time on I never saw Meatloaf return to the hotel in a condition that was any livelier: he must have spent every ounce of energy he had on performing.

The only other group I admired was U2. In fairness I loved their music so I was probably biased, but their arrival and the behaviour of their security team really impressed me. We had quite a lot of fans outside the hotel, and as usual had trouble keeping them away from the front steps. I was on duty with a couple of contract lads for support, and as the coach swept in several fans broke free from their roped holding space and surged forward towards the coach. We all reacted, but their security team, all big guys, jumped down from the moving coach and used a few very strong expletives with enough feeling to stop the fans in their tracks. As I was employed by the hotel, and there wasn't an immediate threat to anyone, I couldn't use physical force against fans, but these guys left the idiots who'd surged towards the coach in no doubt as to the condition they'd be left in if they continued to push forward. I admired that in a security team! Anyway, we moved the over-excited fans back, and helped to keep the rest at bay, enabling the group to move safely into the hotel and up to their rooms. Shortly after this their head of security, Brian, came down to thank us for our help. Now that was practically unheard of. By the end of the band's stay we'd discovered we had the same sense of humour, detested the paparazzi and had little time for mindless autograph hunters – all of which meant we worked really well together. When they left I was extremely sorry to see them go: they were one of the most professional security teams I'd worked with. On the last day I was surprised when Brian offered me a backstage pass for the show that night, enabling me to see how the team operated during a live performance. I'd love to have taken up the offer, but unfortunately we had a group of rappers in later that day, which was never good news.

Personally, I hate rap. Any rap group that has stayed in a hotel where I worked has been nothing but bad news. This included drugs being openly taken in the reception areas and threats to kill. During a visit by 50 Cent I was punched in the kidneys by one of his own people: I really appreciated that when I was trying to keep him safe by ensuring the unknown masses stayed out of the hotel. I even had one of his guys screaming in my ear that if I didn't let the baying crowds in, he'd shoot me! When I refused and told him to 'go away', he marched up the stairs to the bar saying that he was going to 'get that woman shot'. How brave!

Snoop Dogg was possibly slightly better. He came and went with no problems that could be directly linked to him. But as for the people surrounding him – Snoop Dogg, they ain't doing you any favours …

***

Such was security life at hotels. My direct responsibility was always to the hotel, its guests, staff and property. Responsibility for the safe arrival and departure of VIPs lay with the security team associated with them, and this could be rather hit and miss, depending on the professionalism or otherwise of the different security teams. Before the arrival of a VIP group I would carry out a security audit and risk assessments for the visit. This nearly always included an increased costing for additional security cover, depending on the identified threat level. After I'd done all this, I'd present it to the general manager, who'd then inevitably refuse any additional security costs because of 'budget' (a word hated by all hotel staff!). There would then be long and arduous meetings with the general manager, sales manager, conference and banqueting manager, reception manager, and just about any other manager whose department was linked to the arrival – all of them really! Eventually it would be decided (all final decisions being made by the general manager) what additional expenditure would actually be allocated for extra security cover. It was all very laborious and frustrating. Apart from crowd control, decisions also had to involve whether we would actually need door control (yeah, right!); if there was to be open access for everyone, or limited access to non-residents for the spa, bar and restaurant; no access to non-residents at all; a complete close down of the hotel; or any other combination that wouldn't interfere with the hotel outlets making money!

Having done all this, most general managers would then refuse to spend any more on additional security, and I'd be left wondering why I bothered. Somehow, amid all this madness, we'd finally manage to agree to a more or less reasonable compromise, I'd put in place the necessary arrangements, and all would appear to be under control. Until the group arrived – then all carefully laid plans and agreements usually disappeared completely. To quote a well-known military expression, 'No battle plan survives contact with the enemy.' The wonderful thing about being a general manager, or operations manager, is that they were never there at the point of contact. Why should they be? They'd agreed all the operational procedures, the appropriate heads of departments would be in place, so how could anything go wrong? But it often did. It did because at night, or in the early hours of the morning (which was usually when touring coaches arrived following a gig), there were often fewer staff on duty (budget!), and we were usually dealing with extremely large numbers of people with only a handful of security staff to control them (budget!). What seemed reasonable to a general manager during daytime meetings wasn't necessarily going to seem reasonable to an idolised boy/girl band who thought of themselves as gods. Many genuinely believed that if they wanted to invite sixty to eighty 'friends' or fans back to the hotel for a last drink, they should be allowed to. The fact that the residents' bar would be full of guests trying to enjoy a quiet evening drink wouldn't enter their heads.

The results of the above were inevitable. You made decisions on the night that hadn't been agreed at meetings (mainly because safety and security would be breached if you didn't), and got dragged before the general manager the following morning because you'd upset someone and not stuck to an agreed procedure. It's amazing how many people the next day (when they were sober and suited) could plead victimisation by security staff, when the previous night they were drunk and spitting in our faces because we wouldn't comply with their unreasonable demands. Of course when it comes to believing who's right and who's wrong, who's telling the truth and who isn't – you guessed it, it's irrelevant, because the client's never wrong.

That's not to say that I didn't make mistakes. I remember stopping Chris de Burgh coming into a busy hotel one night because he didn't have a resident's card. I just didn't recognise him. He was a resident, and I suppose when you're Chris de Burgh you don't expect security to question why you want to return to your hotel. Luckily Bill was on duty with me at the same time, and as I was blocking the singer's way and asking for proof of identity, he was hissing 'It's Chris de Burgh', his voice getting louder and louder until probably everyone within a hundred yard radius could hear him, except me. Luckily Mr de Burgh thought the situation was amusing.

I'm probably only partially to blame for not recognising the son of a member of a world-famous Liverpool group. The hotel hadn't been informed of his arrival, and not being a fan of the now disbanded group, I knew very little about their families or names of their children. I knew their now deceased lead singer had a famous son because a song had been dedicated to him, but knew nothing about his second son. The first time I heard about his presence was when I got a radio call in the early hours from the night managers, asking me to go to the bar, because there'd been a 'kick off'.

When I arrived both night managers were there, had calmed the situation down and were talking to a group of two male and three female Asians. I'd seen one of the men earlier in the evening trying unsuccessfully to book a room in the hotel, so wondered briefly what he was doing in our residents' bar at 2.20am. As there appeared to be no immediate threat to anyone, I stepped back. I worked very closely with the night managers, and had a lot of respect for them and their capabilities. I also had an agreement with them that I wouldn't interfere with a situation they were already handling, unless there was a threat of aggression or violence.

When the situation appeared to have died down the night managers left, and I walked over to the bar staff to ask what the problem had been. They'd replied that a man sitting at a table near the window was the son of a famous musician. For some reason, and uninvited, the famous son had joined the two Asian men at the bar, and at some point during their conversation had asked them if they knew who he was. Unfortunately one of the two men had replied, 'I don't give a fuck who you are.' Although this seemed like an appropriate reply to me, it had upset the lad, and an argument broke out. When I asked who had escalated the problem, he replied, 'Probably 50/50. They're all drunk anyway.'

As we were talking, the son left the bar and the situation seemed to be over. Unfortunately, five minutes later he reappeared, this time with his bodyguard and another big guy I hadn't seen before. Presumably feeling a lot braver now he had back-up (I've no idea why his bodyguard hadn't been with him earlier!), he started to goad the Asian men, walking past them as close as he could, attempting to make eye contact.

Just as I was wondering if things were about to kick off again, the bodyguard walked over to me and told me his client had complained that he'd now been threatened by the other two men. As it was obvious that his client was the person who wanted to escalate the situation, and as the two Asian men were now sitting quietly at a table talking to their female colleagues, I told him that I'd not been made aware that anyone had threatened him. I pointed out that, in my opinion, as everything seemed to have calmed down it would be better left as it was. The bodyguard happily accepted this, but it soon became obvious that the people with him weren't prepared to.

A few minutes later the bodyguard came back. He said he believed the Asian men weren't residents, and that they should be told to leave as they were breaking the hotel's licensing law. Now I'm a patient person, but this guy had seriously begun to annoy me. I very much doubted if he had a clue about licensing laws, and he obviously wasn't very good at his job. No matter how much he wanted to impress his client, looking at the size of the two Asians, he'd be putting him in harm's way if the situation flared up again. No bodyguard worth their salary would ever do that. I suggested again that as everyone had settled down he leave the situation as it was.

I was then called away to another incident, so left the bar hoping they would all be sensible.

Shortly afterwards a member of the bar staff came to find me, to let me know there'd been another set-to between the two groups. I was beginning to get fed up with the obviously self-opinionated group. I've never had time for people, no matter who they are, who try to use their status, rank or famous name to get their own way, or to dominate a situation. But I knew this problem wasn't going to go away, so I asked the staff member to fill me in on what had happened. He told me that one of the Asians had raised a bottle towards the bodyguard's client, saying that he'd use it on him if he didn't go away. In fairness, this changed things. It certainly wasn't acceptable that someone should be threatened in such a way, no matter how annoying they were.

As I spoke to the barman, I saw two women from the group go over to one of the night managers who'd just walked into the bar, and start to tell him they weren't satisfied thatthe Asians were still in the hotel – and that 'someone's life has been threatened'. This was a bit over the top. One of the women began to get worked up, and demanded that the police be called. The night manager told her she had every right to speak to the police, but that as she was the complainant it would have to be someone from her party who made the official complaint. I could see where this was going, and although I believed the situation wouldn't have arisen if their young colleague hadn't gone over to the two Asians in the first place, or got upset when they didn't know who he was, a threat of violence had been made and had to be dealt with. Checks had confirmed that none of the five Asian were residents, so they had to go.

The night manager raised his eyebrow to me, so I walked over to the Asian group, told them who I was and that an official complaint had been made about threatening behaviour from one of them, and I was therefore asking them to leave the hotel. Both men then informed me that they were residents. I replied that they weren't, and asked them again to leave. This was a worn-out record as far as I was concerned. If I had a pound for every time I've had the same conversation with drunks in a hotel bar in the early hours of the morning, I'd be a very rich lady by now! We went down the usual line of 'Do you know how much I've spent in your bar tonight?' and 'Listen, darling, do you know who I am?' (how I hate that expression!) to 'You're the ugliest woman I've ever seen' (possibly true, but insults and abuse ceased to bother me years ago). As usual, both males refused to leave the hotel, so as usual I informed them that I was removing their right to be there, that a continued refusal to leave would result in their being classed as trespassers, and that I was sure they wouldn't want the police to respond to this. One of the men finally said, 'I'll leave when I've finished my drink.' As his glass was empty I replied, 'That'll be now then,' and to my surprise he answered, 'OK, I'm going.' I usually have to push a lot harder than that!

Eventually, after a lot of abuse, and a surprising amount of support from their three companions (I think even the girls had had enough of them by now), the men began to move towards the main staircase leading to reception and the way out. They'd just reached the top of the stairs when the taller man suddenly produced his mobile phone, and began screaming into it, 'There's a Susan Jones throwing us out of the hotel. Get down here and sort it out.' To this day I have no idea who he was talking to – possibly just himself in an attempt to frighten me! However, as they continued down the stairs I followed at a distance, trying not to wind them up still further. Just as we reached reception the taller man (the smaller one seemed to have exhausted his repertoire of threats and insults and had sunk into a drunken stumble) suddenly stopped and said, 'I'm not leaving the hotel.' I was getting tired by now, so I pointed out his choices: to go at my request or go at the insistence of the police. I didn't care either way. Again to my surprise, one of the women turned to him and said, 'You're going. You've been disgusting.' I assumed the argument was going to kick off again, so I was amazed when the group turned and left the hotel together.

By the time I got back to the bar wonder boy and his bodyguard had disappeared, presumably back to their rooms and hopefully to sleep. At least two hours had been wasted just because someone wanted someone else to know who he was. How sad is that?

My ghosts have left me alone for quite a while now, but thinking of bodyguards raises an old memory.

*London. Harrods is crowded. Hoards of people obsessed with shopping seem to be moving in the opposite direction to us. I wonder how the woman in front of me can take so much buffeting without wanting to leave the store and get a taxi back to the hotel. I ask her again if she is OK with the crowds, but she merely flicks her eyes towards me, then moves off once more in the direction of the dress section. I groan inwardly: we have been there at least three times already. There's only the two of us, and I realised hours ago that if someone was trailing us, or wanted to injure or kill the woman with me, I have little or no hope of stopping them. Knowing the high profile of this lady's husband I'd suggested more than one bodyguard, but the request had been denied.*

*The women's clothing area seems less crowded, and this obviously delights my charge, who moves from rail to rail pulling clothes hangers apart to look more closely at the expensive garments hanging on them. I glance around the area for the hundredth time, and wonder why my head zooms back to a couple, both male, several yards from us. Maybe it's because they are both men in a dress section; equally they could be picking something for their mother or sister. They don't look over in our direction, but the intense scrutiny of the clothes they are looking at seems just a little too staged. The hairs on the back of my neck stand up. Why? I pretend to be looking at a scarf, holding it up to the light so that I can see past it to the men beyond. Nothing. I glance at the woman with me. She is holding several hangers draped with clothes: any minute now she will head to the changing rooms, not a place I want her to go at the moment. I look back at my scarf and the two unknowns. Nothing. Then, suddenly, a minute movement of the head, an assessment of direction; the direction of my client. I drop the scarf and move quickly to her side. 'Time to go,' I tell her. I take the coat hangers from her and drape them over the nearest rail. She looks at me as if I've lost my senses. 'Coffee time,' I say in a loud voice, 'a couple of floors up, just what we need; we can come back for those later.' Her mouth moves to speak, but I interrupt. 'Now!'*

*Probably for the first time since we met she actually looks me in the eye. Her eyes open wide, and her face changes colour. But I'm not waiting for conversation. I take her by the arm and direct her towards the main staircase – safer than the lifts. I don't look back, but talking rubbish all the while I use every mirror and shiny surface to try and see what the men are doing. I can see nothing. We eventually come out on the ground floor. Hopefully a taxi will be outside. I take one quick look around, see nothing, so still holding her arm I march her straight out of the store and into a black cab. Giving the name of a central hotel, I turn to look out of* the back window. There is nothing to see. No cabs pull out after us. I turn to apologise to the lady with me, but she turns away with a brusque comment I don't catch. I presume she is annoyed with me for spoiling her afternoon's shopping. But I believe my actions were correct; it's the late 1980s, radios are not always supplied as standard issue, nor mobile phones to summon assistance or to check identities. There is silence in the cab until we get to the hotel I had asked for. There is still nothing behind us. As the cab slows I lean forward and give the driver the name of the hotel we actually want. He doesn't seem too amused to be messed around.

Twenty minutes later we turn into the road leading to the hotel. 'I want to walk from here,' the lady informs the driver, without asking my opinion. There's nothing behind us, and I see the hotel in the distance. I can see no threat, and she's the boss. We leave the taxi and begin to walk along the tree-lined street. A short distance from the hotel two men appear around the corner. I recognise both of them. I'm not armed; I can't carry a firearm in the UK. I move slightly in front of her. We have to continue to move forward; there's nowhere else to go. As the distance closes between us one of the men moves off the pavement, the other continuing straight towards us. 'Keep walking,' I say to her. 'No matter what happens, keep walking straight into that hotel, straight to reception and get hotel security to take you to your room.' The single male is no more than a couple of paces in front of us. He hasn't veered in any way from his path, and is on collision course with us: his eyes are fixed on the woman with me. His left hand moves to his pocket. When we're no more than a couple of paces apart I shoot forward, my right hand grabs the left-hand side of his lapel and my left hand grabs his right shoulder. I push violently with my right, while pulling equally violently with my left hand, then shove. I've only used the technique in training, but it works well. The man flies off the pavement to his left, immobilising his left-hand side and cannoning into his companion. I have my ward through and running into the hotel. I expect the crack of a gun, or the impact of a bullet, even a shout, but there is nothing. When I turn on the steps both men have gone. I have no idea who they are, or what they wanted.

## CHAPTER SIXTEEN
# TRAINING AND PERSONALITY CLASHES

Hotels create large amounts of intense emotion and passion, both in guests who use them and staff who work in them. And, in my opinion, large quantities of emotion and passion are never a good thing!

I think it's true to say that many people employed in hotels are extremely hard working and care deeply about the standards they work to and the service they provide. Having said that, there are equally staff who care little for anything, apart from removing items of hotel property without authority to do so, and doing as little as possible without actually getting sacked.

It's undeniable that staff work ridiculously long hours for little pay and equally little thanks, and although it's their choice to work in hotels this inevitably leads to frustration, resentment and anger. A melting pot of all these emotions in the workplace is usually a recipe for disaster, and can only ever lead to dramatic and fiery scenes, arguments and, eventually, clashes of character.

One other small problem with working in hotels is that few members of staff actually tell the truth. Take the truth behind training, for instance. Now I've probably attended dozens, literally dozens, of staff training sessions, and worse still staff training days. They're false, geared towards the terminally stupid, never get any better, and are filled with such mind-boggling quotes as this one, from a once world-famous hotelier: 'It has been and continues to be, our responsibility to fill the earth with the light and warmth of hospitality.' Now, if that doesn't make you feel nauseous, nothing will. Running a hotel is purely and simply about making money – no matter what they tell you.

Until my dying day I'll continue to tell people that working in a hotel is nothing but hard work, something akin to forced labour, and that temperaments are such that clashes among staff, and sometimes with guests, are to be expected. Of course I usually add that if you've been bitten by the hotel bug you're not going to be able to walk away from it all.

I remember the first hotel training session I attended in Liverpool. My training up to that moment had consisted mainly of such things as martial arts, unarmed combat, assault courses and live ammunition firearms drills before breakfast. Like the innocent I was, I looked forward to my new training, and went jogging for an hour before work to clear the cobwebs and get my mind focused on this new venture.

A memory interrupts.

*The old house has no heating, and it's freezing. I'll be glad to get out on the assault course; at least I'll be warm. I dress quickly, then pull aside the old curtain separating me from the lads. I creep past their beds, making it to the steps that lead down to the kitchen without waking anyone. First rule of the team; if you're up first you make the brew. I'm only glad I don't have to cook breakfast. No-one stirs as I walk into the grey kitchen. Three enormous bowls of cereal have been left out for us, together with loaves of bread and jars of tea and coffee. I stick the kettle on, then pick up a dish to scoop cereal into. I go for the cornflakes bowl, and my heart nearly stops when two green eyes peer out at me from the bowl rim. A large black and white cat is curled up on top of the flakes. To its complete disgust I pick it up and throw it out, then go back to remove the top layer of cat hair from the cereal. No need for the lads to know.*

Memories never come one at a time.

*Three doors lead off the corridor. The Killing House is damp and eerie, and it feels good to have a firearm in my hand. In a few seconds I have to choose which door to enter, and nothing interrupts the silence to help me decide which one I will pick. It's probably irrelevant; all the rooms have to be checked anyway. I pick the one nearest to me; at least I'll know the section of house behind me is clear. The room is empty. The next two doors are more or less opposite each other, so I choose the left-hand one. I fling open the door and immediately see a mother with a pram standing in front of me, to their right I see the dark shape of a male figure. His weapon is raised and aimed at her. I shoot him.*

*'Cease fire, lower weapon – oh man, Sue, you've shot the photographer again!' My trainer walks from behind me to examine the cardboard cutout of a dark coated photographer. 'Hmm, two chest shots. Pity you shot the wrong person.' I look at the figure I've shot. I should have known it wouldn't be straight forward, it never is – that's the point of training. The figure looks as if he has a gun raised, but in fact what I took for a weapon is a camera. 'You horrible person,' my trainer continues. 'There was the loving husband taking a photograph of his adored wife and baby, and you come bursting in and shoot him!' He laughs, then turns more serious. 'Go and have a look at the pram'. I walk over, knowing what I will see, and am not surprised that there's no sign of a plastic baby. The pram is full of assault rifles, plastic grenades and large round black objects with 'bomb' written on them. 'You always have to know what you're looking at. Identify the real threat. This lot were obviously terrorists making mementos, or putting together propaganda photos. You should have shot both of them.'*

By lunchtime of my first hotel training session I was bored beyond reason. Without stop, the apparently mindless female 'trainers' had chirruped and chirped away like a couple of demented doves. The only eventual advantage to this forced drivel was that when they inevitably put us together in pairs to 'bond', I was placed with the then front of house manager, Colette Brannan, a very professional lady who already had managerial experience within hotels. She would teach me a lot about them over the next five years. It turned out Colette was also unimpressed with the training and trainers – and our mutual loathing became the basis of a long and lasting friendship, which helped us both stay sane during our years in Liverpool.

By the end of the two-day course that our well-known hotel had put on to enlighten us as to why we wanted to work in hotels, I was convinced that I'd been unlucky with the selection of trainers they'd supplied. I was wrong, of course: training like this continued in the same vein no matter which hotel group I worked for. These sessions were supposed to allow staff the opportunity (when the chirruping and chirping had stopped) to talk honestly about their frustrations and concerns, voice their opinions about specific training they felt they needed, and to be open and truthful about their roles – if they were brave enough to do so! In a lot of cases telling the truth, the whole truth and nothing but the truth would probably have cost them their jobs. That's why most hotel staff lie, and of course this could and usually did lead to clashes of character – often involving a general manager somewhere along the line.

My last hotel was in Manchester. I knew after working there for eighteen months that I really wasn't crazy enough to want more. The only way I could describe that hotel would be to call it a complete and utter madhouse. And here's the interesting thing: it shouldn't have been. No-one who worked there could ever work out why staff left its employment gibbering and twitching: they just did. The hotel had a very strong general manager, who was an ardent believer in training. In fairness, the fact that yet again training was under par wasn't her fault. The hotel chain demanded high standards from its staff, and this involved high levels of training; unfortunately, no-one ever seemed to stand back and ask if this instruction was good or extremely poor. Training was mandatory, so I attended all the sessions and ran several myself: it was part of my job. But as the training I delivered involved crisis, terrorist threat, fire and evacuation, most members of staff swallowed hard before they came in, remained silent throughout and left as soon as I'd finished. No one wants to be reminded what could happen to their nice, safe hotel if a devastating crisis should occur. They certainly don't want to think what would happen if terrorists attacked the hotel with automatic weapons and grenades, as happened in the Taj Mahal Palace and Oberoi Trident hotels in Mumbai in November 2008. Most staff wanted to get out of training sessions as fast as possible, and many saw them just as a rest or a change from their daily duties.

Another ghost forces a memory.

*The revolver seems ungainly in my hand; strange because it is a lighter weapon than the Colt I usually carry. The property is big, silent and empty. Empty apart from the one person I know to be in there. I can hear my heart thumping: it sounds so loud that I'm sure the whole house must hear it. The door in front of me is half open, but a quick check above it reveals the booby-trap device. I back away and move further down the corridor; there could be another door. There is, and I enter as silently and as cautiously as I can. I make a rapid, visual assessment of the room; near, far, high, low, 'clear'. The next room and the kitchen are all clear. I pause to listen, but all I can hear is my own heartbeat. I know he's in here, and I know he has a firearm. He's good, but then he should be. There's one more floor to go. I place my foot gently on the first step and slowly begin to mount the stairs. First room; clear. Second room; clear. The door to the third room is slightly ajar. Too late I see the disturbed dust particles descending to settle on the floor. A fraction of movement above and to my right. I throw myself forward, shooting as I fall; but I'm not quick enough, and even before I pull my trigger I hear the sharp report of another weapon being discharged. He fires from his position nestled into the ceiling above, and there is a tremendous 'whack' to the top of my thigh as he accurately 'takes me out'.*

*'Time: lower and make weapons safe.' My trainer is behind me. 'You OK?' he asks. 'Yes, no problems,' I reply, thinking, 'I hope at least one of my rounds got him'. Pete Scholey drops from the ceiling. 'Both your rounds whistled just above my head. Bit lower and I'd have been cross eyed.' I think of the wax bullets we'd been training with; he'd have been*

*more than cross eyed, he'd probably have had a hole big enough for a third eye. I leave the house determined not to limp!*

Now that training I really enjoyed!

One of the staff members I worked with in Manchester was an executive chef called David Gale, a truly outstanding character, for whom I had nothing but respect. When he attended a training session this respect soared to absolute admiration, because David always told the truth. He was passionate about everything that went on in his kitchens, his food, the service, the attitude of his staff, and like most executive chefs had an opinion that was going to be heard no matter what. But what I really admired about David was his willingness to challenge anything, in fact everything that went on in the hotel, and that included training. Every now and then we'd have a staff training day, which involved the usual corporate training team (in this hotel a man and a woman), who skipped into the training room, acted as if they were talking to kindergarten kids, clapped their hands and told everyone how wonderful it was to work for the hotel, how we'd have a great day because we'd make it fun, we'd play games and we'd bond as a team. Yeah, right. When these apparently constantly happy adults took us for any sort of training I'd look at David, and he'd look at me, and I'd wonder who hated them more!

One particular day all heads of departments (HoDs) had attended mandatory training, at the end of which, yet again, I believed I had achieved nothing. It had been a long boring day, and I'd only kept awake by mentally planning the demise of the two instructors several times, each demise being nastier and more painful than the last. Finally, after the end of a day of character assessment (more like assassination), team bonding and group 'games' we were told to return to our seats. I sat down heavily on mine, genuinely confused as to how any of this nonsense had made us better people or managers. While we relaxed in our seats, our female instructor prattled away, finally announcing that it was time for our comments about the course. She informed us that she would ask each HoD individually (presumably just in case we got carried away with the excitement of the day and all spoke at once) for our views on the training. We could then let everyone know how we would set about taking that training back to our departments, to share with our colleagues.

'Now I want you all to be honest,' she beamed, her head on one side as if reassuring a class of fearful children. 'We can all be confident in our new selves and in the knowledge we've gained. We can speak the truth, learn from today's team building, and, moving forward [how I hate that expression], become better and more organised people and departments.' She breathed deeply, clasping her hands in what appeared to be an ecstasy of self-satisfaction. It gave the feeling that you should all be on your feet hugging the brand flag and rejoicing in our new understanding of the true meaning of service and standards.

I glanced round the room. Being in the middle facing her, I realised that whether we moved in a clockwise or anti-clockwise direction, I'd be able to listen to at least half my colleagues give their 'honest opinions' before it was my turn. I knew that all replies would be both mindful and fearful of the general manager, who was sitting to one side. I also knew that when it was my turn or David's our answers wouldn't be appreciated by the trainer, and certainly not by the general manager! David sat off to my right: if the instructor chose a clockwise approach to our honest and truthful answers she'd get David's before mine.

I looked back at the trainer who beamed at us all again.

'Now,' she gushed with breathless delight, 'starting from my left, I want you to tell us all what you learned today, and what it is you'll be taking back to your departments.' So off they went, giving the answers they knew were required by both trainer and general manager; mostly untrue, because at least 75 per cent of those present thought the same way as David and I did: the sessions were a complete waste of time, money and effort. I sat back and listened.

'That was really inspirational training, and I can take that inspiration back to my department to ensure all my team benefits from today.' Hmm, not bad, even if it is all lies!

'I feel really focused and refreshed. I now feel confident that the things I've learned today can be shared by my team, and therefore ensure a better service and higher standards than before.' Oh please, you're all starting to sound like politicians!

And so it went around the room: all hastily put together thoughts completely non-reflective of the standard of training, which had been sub-standard to say the least. But it would satisfy the tick-boxes for trainer and general manager alike, and ensure that the HoD in particular hadn't raised his or her head higher than necessary in order to get it shot off!

After seven or eight of these dishonest comments the trainer came to David. She knew him, but the general manager knew him better. Being a good general manager and wanting control at all times, she looked him directly in the eye, non-verbally warning him that he had to play ball and behave nicely.

'So, David,' she said icily, interrupting the trainer. 'What did you learn today, and what will you take back to your department?'

David took her direct and commanding gaze, returned it and calmly replied, 'Fuck all.' I've rarely admired someone so much. Honesty at last!

I think I rephrased it slightly when it came to my turn, but the meaning remained the same. It really didn't matter, because the training representative from that famous brand of hotels was suffering a fit of the vapours and had ceased listening to anyone after that. Just as well David was such a good chef!

While on the subject of chefs, I remember another superb executive chef, Eyck Zimmer. Apart from being recognised at international level for his culinary delights, with a string of awards to his bow, Eyck was well known in the hotel for his openness, honesty and complete lack of tolerance of anything that wasn't perfect.

Eyck's most famous clash within the hotel was with an environmental health officer who'd carried out an inspection on his freezer a couple of months previously, and, finding that some items weren't dated, had marked the inspection down. Eyck was away at the time, but when he returned he was informed of the transgression. Needless to say, he hadn't put the items in the freezer, and with the usual temperament of an executive chef he blasted the poor subordinate responsible. Things calmed down, and a month or so later the same inspector visited the kitchens again. This time Eyck was there, and when the inspector checked the freezer and found items again not dated, Eyck responded by sending all undated packets flying across the kitchen, followed by kitchen racking (which happened to be in the way at the time), followed by the unfortunate soul who was responsible for the misdemeanour (who also happened to be in the way at the time). Not that I'm blaming him: not dating food is how food poisoning occurs. Good for you, Eyck: I wish we all had the courage to do it!

Going back to training, it's possible I'm unfair in criticising the hotels or hotel groups I worked for. I'm sure they believed they were giving staff better training, and therefore providing higher standards of service, happier guests and a reduction in complaints (which was always important to them!). But judging from the fact that every training session I attended was the same, I presumed the hotels were pinching everyone else's training anyway. Perhaps a more open and honest approach, given by someone who threw away the old training sheets, might have been more productive and more appreciated by those attending.

Shortly before I left hotel employment the brand I was with was centralised, in that everything was directed by their American head office and had therefore turned American. Now I'm sure that worked in their American hotels, but it didn't go down too well in Britain, where there was a different market and different requirements. But that didn't stop them putting us through the same training.

As a follow-on to monthly HoD meetings, the general manager showed us training videos to help us improve our standards of service, or rather how they did it American-style, then let us loose in our departments to filter these sessions down to our own people. It had an amazing effect. Everyone started to go round talking with American accents. Reception staff started to put their right hands across their hearts when they couldn't give a guest the room he or she wanted, and came out with such drivel as 'Gee, Mrs Whatever, I'm so sorry. I see from our records that during your last visit you preferred room 231.

Unfortunately we've booked it out to another guest, but knowing your requirements I'd be happy to offer you room 321, which is exactly the same as your preferred room, just on another floor.' Guests started to look at receptionists as if they were making fun of them. They weren't used to it. Not even our American guests. It just wasn't British, and in some cases I believe we actually annoyed people. Imagine a busy check-in period, with guests lined up, all impatient to get to the receptionist, fill in the paperwork, have their credit cards swiped and, most importantly, get to their room. They were more used to 'I'm sorry, that room's not available. Can I offer you another?' Now surely that's better. It says it all quicker and more precisely. Guests really didn't want to wait, tired and hot after their journey, then have to listen to a receptionist prattle away to three or four other guests queuing in front of them. They found it frustrating enough to queue at all. Anyway, with one hand over the heart it was awkward for receptionists to operate the computers!

***

I suppose it's no wonder that, among the living machinery that is a hotel, personality clashes are bound to occur on a regular basis. I always genuinely believed that if you had a good, strong, professional general manager in charge, things would operate a lot more smoothly than if you had one interested only in profit and their own rise to fame. Sometimes the trouble was finding a good GM to work for, because if you clashed with the GM the end result was predictable: you weren't going to be the winner!

I don't think I've upset too many GMs in my time, with the exception of the one in Liverpool, that is! As I've said, he and I only seriously clashed after I told him that I believed his involvement with prostitutes threatened the security of the hotel, and possibly the whole company – something he never forgave me for. Up until that time we'd managed to circle each other without major conflict, but this changed one day when he asked me to attend a meeting, 'just between the two of us', supposedly to discuss a hotel security review. The review was never raised, and the meeting turned into a major clash when he suddenly started asking me what my wardrobe was like at home. He said he bet it was tidy with neat sections for suits, skirts, blouses and so on. Now I'd never met anyone with a wardrobe fetish before, and I wasn't sure how to handle this comment, so I'd replied that my wardrobe was extremely untidy – and that the last time I lost the cat I'd found her in there forty-eight hours later. Foolishly, I thought that would be the end of it, but he obviously didn't share my sense of humour. 'Nobody knows who you are. Nobody knows the real Sue Jones. You know too much.'

By this time I knew that a parting of the ways was inevitable. As far as I was concerned, my home life stayed at the front doors of the hotel when I walked in at the start of each shift, and I didn't pick it up again until I left at the end of my shift. I also knew that this clash was about to become terminal because I believed the general manager was a complete fool, and he obviously thought I was someone who had tidy wardrobes and knew too much. He continued with, 'You're an ice maiden. You build up walls between yourself and other people. People see Sue Jones in work, but they don't know the real Sue Jones.'

I can repeat these words exactly thanks to Pitman and my ability to write everything down in shorthand. I always took notes during meetings with this particular manager, then went back to my office, transcribed the text and typed it up within an hour of our meeting; then I'd send him a copy just to annoy him. In fact, I kept records of every meeting I ever attended over forty years: the house groans under the weight!

I wasn't the only one to clash with that general manager, of course. Colette probably had more disagreements with him than I did, although that's debatable. I believe we were both strong managers, who questioned decisions and procedures if they didn't make sense to us. I also believed that as managers responsible for our departments this was what our roles required of us. I often wondered if that bothered the general manager. Certainly he appeared to try very hard to have us moved on, although by the time he turned his attention to

Colette she was already a general manager in her own right – so this made it difficult for him to achieve this goal.

I remember a disciplinary meeting the man held against Colette for some misdemeanour or other. At the time he'd risen to the dizzy heights of group general manager, so his sense of power had no limits. He very properly arranged a meeting with himself, the HR manager and Colette. Being able to take a work colleague with her, Colette chose me.

The meeting revolved around Colette being in the hotel one evening and supposedly making a derogatory comment about the hotel's management team. This was reported back to the general manager, who took exception to it. It was all very complicated and extremely childish. During the meeting Colette was completely confused as to what the GM was talking about, and after an equally confusing exchange between the two of them about the incident (which I certainly found hard to follow, but duly wrote down in shorthand), the GM asked us to leave the room, saying he'd send for us when he was ready to give his verdict. It sounded like the beginning of a sentence for hanging! Approximately twenty minutes later we were summoned to return, and I walked into the room expecting to see him with a black handkerchief on his head. If we'd been confused earlier, his opening comments lost us both completely. Word for word it went like this, with no pause for punctuation, and hardly a gasp for breath.

> My concerns are that as I go through the statements there is a common thread that suggests to me a behaviour that I am not comfortable with and that reflects around the fact that I don't see a respect for the management of this hotel and a respect for the rest of the managers within the company [quick intake of breath] and that is the biggest issue as far as I am concerned and moving forward if I felt that there was an acceptance that you had got it wrong and maybe you could have done it

better in a better way then my view of what took place is one of well I am right and you can do whatever you like. This is a big issue and I don't know if I feel that you feel this.

By this time I was exhausted at trying to work out exactly what was being said, while writing it down in shorthand at the same time. Colette was studying the ceiling with a confused expression on her face, and the GM had turned purple and was trying very hard to gather air into his lungs. There was a long pause, then he continued:

On those grounds there has been a previous discussion with behaviour around this and I would take the opportunity to take it very seriously [quick intake of breath] and my decision would be I will record a verbal warning on how you were conducting conversations within the hotel [slightly longer pause for breath]. If I believe that you are of that opinion then I am comfortable with that there is no benefit I see in just serving out written warnings I don't think that is the way of dealing with a senior manager of the hotel [short intake of breath] and I will take your word that you accept that that was not the right way of doing it and I am comfortable that this is the right level of sanction [a final and deep breath]. If you feel that you have been unjustly treated you have the right of appeal. That is to the Director of Operations, and that is within seven working days.

And that was the end of the meeting.

When we left the room a few minutes later Colette stopped. 'Do you have any idea what he was talking about?' she asked.

'Nope, not a clue. Not even sure if he did. He seemed very nervous about the whole thing. I think there was possibly a verbal warning in there, but I'm not sure what for.'

Colette looked puzzled for a few seconds. 'Come to think about it, neither am I. Oh well, no doubt he'll write and let me know. Let's go and get coffee.'

I imagine the general manager felt he won this particular battle, because in the end he wrote a letter to Colette giving her a written warning. She naturally appealed against it, attaching a copy of my notes, and I have a feeling the charge was dropped. In my case the general manager believed he'd won the contest, because he made me redundant shortly afterwards. Actually, I think I won, because I moved to London, and a really great hotel – and I liked the GM too!

I suppose that when you sum it all up there are no winners when two people clash like that, merely more experienced combatants. Eventually you take your frustrations and anger to your next role, and possibly the next. And that doesn't satisfy anyone, because you don't get the opportunity, or the time, to get rid of those frustrations or angers. You're too busy building up new ones!

# CHAPTER SEVENTEEN
# THE LAST DEMON

Years later I looked back and wondered what I'd learned from Liverpool, London and Manchester, and the time I'd spent working in those cities. The sad thing was I couldn't think of much. I missed the teams of lads I'd worked with. I missed their loyalty and bravery, the camaraderie and the great fun we had together. I missed that feeling in the early hours in the morning after we'd combined our knowledge and experience, and nobody had got shot, or died, or was even seriously injured. I missed working until three or four in the morning, then driving back home with the sun slowly coming up and nothing but birds and sunlight for company. But gaining strength and knowledge through learning new and interesting things, as I'd done in close protection and when I worked as a risk and security consultant with my own business ... no, I couldn't think of anything. I could only remember frustration, annoyance and a feeling of waste. I found that really sad.

It occurred to me that maybe I was just getting older, and that was a frightening thought. Personally I felt no different from how I had in my twenties, but my knees, back and mirror told me otherwise. I didn't leap out of bed in the morning any more: I contemplated the move thoughtfully, and certainly without the excitement I used to have at the start of a new day. There were certain exercises I wouldn't even attempt any more, while running was something my imagination did without me physically supporting the idea, and walks in the mountains involved the car covering a greater distance than I did.

I found myself going around humming the tune to a favourite song of mine. It questioned the use of the human spirit outlasting physical strength, particularly when that physical strength failed through illness or age. How apt that song would become. It wasn't that I was ready to give it all up, but I was up to my armpits in cynicism, scepticism and an extremely low tolerance level toward my fellow human beings.

Although my ghosts had left me alone for quite a while now, a final one surfaced, and I remembered a winter's evening nearly forty years ago – and a conversation I'd had with a complete stranger on the banks of the Moose river at the bottom of James Bay in Canada.

*The last flashes of violent colour from the evening sky are magnified in the wide river in front of me; in less than an hour it will be pitch black. My boots crunch on the shingle beach and I know that in a couple of minutes the cold will send me back to my vehicle. I'm aware that for the last twenty minutes or so I've not been alone; unusual for this location and this time of year. The figure looks male, although it's difficult to tell with the thick fur-hooded parka that he's wearing. I feel no threat, and am not surprised when he moves closer. When he speaks his dialect is broad, and I'm not sure what he's said, although he's looking at the sky and its brilliant display. I gaze at him once more and believe he's of Inuit descent. He speaks again, and talks about being further south than he'd like to be at this time of the year, and although our meeting is completely random, we begin to talk as if we've known each other for a lifetime. As the light starts to fade we discuss much, even though his accent means I sometimes struggle to understand all he is saying. I've never known how it can happen that you meet a complete stranger, and within minutes you're talking as if lifelong friends. But from personal experience I know that every now and then it does happen, and when it does, the impact of that meeting can change your perception of life forever.*

*He listens without interruption to my reasons for being out in Canada at that time of the year, travel (as always) allowing me escape. Then he talks about his journey; a journey he takes every year because his father had taken the same journey, and his father's father before him. There is a long, comfortable pause, both of us immersed in the beauty of the evening. Then slowly he starts talking again, as if continuing a mental conversation he's been holding with himself. He talks about gifts we should give ourselves, and that I should give myself three. The first being time; the second the gift of understanding, for myself and others; and the third to use a gift he says I already have, 'telling stories'. 'You should write these down,' he says.*

I'd like to think that this meeting played a part in my deciding to write when I finally turned my back on security and my profession. He was right all those years ago: writing down things that happened to me certainly helped. Thank you, whoever you were.

So much for my ghosts; sometimes I was grateful for their presence and their unpredictable way of presenting memories to confirm and clarify events. Sometimes I hated their interruption. Then I remembered another beach, another stretch of water, and my last demon raises its head to look me in the eye.

*I never have heard from my Royal Naval colleague. The parcel is still with me, and is a complete nuisance. It's been years now since he left it in the boot of my car, and it's time to get rid of it. I'm sure he won't come back, and if he does he'll be disappointed that it doesn't accompany him on his way home. Did he intend me to keep hold of it? Was I supposed to act on it in some way? I doubted it. Anyway, he wouldn't be able to find me now if he tried. Too many moves; too much time has elapsed. I presume there's a reason it was given to me, but if there is I fail to understand what that reason was. A couple of years ago I had lifted a corner of the package to ensure there was nothing obviously illegal about it. It was paperwork as I had thought originally, no drugs, no gems, no weaponry. I hadn't taken the contents out, and the paperwork remained undisturbed.*

*There's a beach on the east side of the Isle of Anglesey; Penmon Point. Remote, windswept and, for most of the winter months, deserted; an old haunt of mine when I lived in North Wales. I take the package there and open it, read the handwritten scripts, and instantly regret any involvement I might now have. Such things belong in Government archives, or in history books, and any newspaper or conspiracy theorist would have paid a fortune for it. Why my naval acquaintance should have had it is beyond me. I look back over the couple of months that I knew him, and the only link I can associate with him lies within the security field. I don't know if that is relevant.*

*Fire is a great destroyer, and I burn every last sheet.*

# CHAPTER EIGHTEEN
# CANADA

October 2010. Bill and I were back in Canada, and as always I felt as if I'd come home. I'd felt that way since I first travelled to the country over forty years earlier, and felt it each time I returned. This time, though, we hadn't come on holiday: we were trying to find a permanent home. With all my demons and ghosts silenced, I was ready to find one.

The snows had arrived early, and the lake in front of us was mostly frozen, its rim hard with ice and snow against the bank. The wind was freezing, and I buried my face into the high neck of my jacket to try and protect it from the cold. Bill was a couple of feet behind me, moving cautiously because of a bad knee. He probably shouldn't have been walking on it at all, but he was stubborn as a mule – and probably moving as slowly as one.

We'd been on the trail for a couple of hours, and I knew we had at least another hour before we got back to the small clearing and the 4x4 waiting for us. The air was so clear and still that I'd felt as if I was the first person to ever walk the trail, and when I moved out of the tree line to drop down to the side of the lake, I stopped, absolutely blown away by the view. The pine trees were frozen in time, sparkling white with frost and snow-laden branches. The lake glittered a million diamonds of silver and blue, and in the distance the high peaks of the Rockies stood as always, silent sentinels to that beautiful land. I waited for Bill, and as he stopped beside me there was no need for words. I knew he felt the same way as I did about it, and that was enough.

'Come on.' He prodded me with his snow stick. 'I'm sure I can smell coffee.' We were still laughing at this absurdity when we moved downhill away from the trees. It was then we saw the prints in the snow. 'Those are big!' said Bill. 'Cat, I believe. Big cat.' He stopped to look round. 'Actually, a very, very big cat!' I dropped down to look closely at the prints. I put my right boot next to the indent, which was alarmingly double the size! 'Cougar or bobcat.' I knew there'd been sightings of cougar nearby. They hadn't been seen here for many years before the previous summer, so I was both thrilled and slightly alarmed. 'Oh well, it's unlikely it'll take on both of us,' I said, trying to appear more confident than I felt. We were after all on its home territory, and definitely part of its food chain! 'We'll just have to make more noise as we walk. You go on in front. Your breathing should frighten anything away.'

A snowball missed my head by inches. 'No, you've got a whistle in your pack. Get it ready; you can blow its ears off if it decides to attack.' I ignored him, unbelievably excited that one of the most beautiful animals in the Rockies could be close by, sitting on its haunches, watching us puff along as noisily as we could.

We continued along the trail. There were several prints, obviously fresh, but whatever kind of cat it was, it certainly wasn't going to let us catch sight of it. We eventually negotiated the last icy hill and walked out of the pines into the clearing, glad to see the 4x4 where we'd left it. I'd often wondered how we'd fare if someone ever stole it and we had to walk to the nearest township. Not that there was anyone around, we'd not seen sight nor sound of anyone since our arrival.

I took off my rucksack and leaned it against the side of the car. It had been a long walk, the temperature was in the region of minus 11, and my body was telling me that I'd probably asked a couple of miles too much of it. Bill didn't look any better. 'Let's drop down into Banff and grab a coffee before we drive back to the cabin,' I suggested. There was a nod from Bill as he bent to pick up a glove he'd dropped. But instead of retrieving the glove and straightening up he remained bent. I was just about to ask if he was OK when I saw the tracks in the snow that he was looking at.

'Wow, it's been around the car as well,' I started to say, but stopped in mid-sentence when I realised they weren't cat prints; they were much bigger.

'Those are bear prints,' Bill said calmly. 'I thought they hibernated up in the mountains this time of year.'

'We *are* up in the mountains,' I answered. 'Quite a way up, actually. Oh, and they don't always hibernate all year round.' Bill straightened and looked around. We both did. I expected at any moment to hear the cough or jaw popping of an angry grizzly, and quickly started looking in my pocket for the car keys. The silence was total apart from the thumping of my heart.

'OK, let's not waste time opening the boot. Just put the stuff in the back seat, and let's get in,' I said, trying to sound calm and in control, even though my body was tense, waiting for the crashing noise the bear would make as it broke through the nearby bushes before shredding us with a swipe of a lethal paw. We flung packs in the back, and ourselves into the front seats seconds later. The safety of the car brought back sanity and calm.

I sighed. Sometimes I hated myself. 'You know I've got to take a picture of those prints, don't you?' I said, looking at Bill, who was slowly removing layer after layer of clothing.

'Fine', he replied. 'You get the camera, then pop outside and take the photograph. I'll stay here and keep watch. In fact, swop over, I'll get into the driver's seat, ready for a quick getaway in case the bear doesn't feel too photogenic.' An opportunity for sarcasm was never lost on Bill. 'We've probably got plenty of time. It's probably chatting away with the cougar as we speak, trying to agree which one of them gets the juicier parts of us.'

But in the car I was full of courage, and anyway, I knew no-one would ever believe us unless I took photographs. 'Perfect,' I replied tartly, 'and you can have the pleasure of explaining to my grandchildren why you allowed their grandmother to go alone into the wilderness to face grizzlies, cougars and a host of other starving, prowling beasts, without giving her some form of back-up.'

'Oh, I'll give you back-up,' replied Bill. 'I'll leave the door open. Well, I'll leave it open until the bear or cougar attacks, and then, believe me, I'm going to shut it very quickly again, whether or not you're in the car.'

Muttering scathing comments under my breath I picked up the camera, zipped my jacket up and stepped out into the snow. My door remained open, but I saw Bill move across ready to close it. Great, I thought, such loyalty!

I was amazed again at the beauty and silence of that stunning place, even as I took the photographs. Perhaps it was so silent because a predator was near, and all intelligent animals were quiet, not wanting to draw attention to themselves. The camera seemed to make awfully loud clicks, but I walked round the vehicle taking pictures, measuring the prints against my boot, which sank into insignificance against the paw marks next to it. In a few minutes I was back in the car, heart racing a bit if I was honest, but delightedly holding my trophy in the camera.

'You know,' I said, 'if we hold on here for an hour or two, we might even see the animal that made those prints. That would be incredible. I've been coming to this spot for years, and I've never seen a bear around here. Just about everything else, but never a bear, nor a cougar. Wouldn't that be great?'

'Wonderful,' Bill replied dryly, 'but it's getting late, I'm dying for a coffee and it's starting to snow again. It's time to go.'

He was right, of course. Despite the warmth of the car I had started to shiver, and there was at least an hour to drive before we reached civilisation. I bent forward to untie the top laces of my snow boots. For some reason the fingers on my left hand wouldn't work. Thinking it was the cold, I blew warm air onto them. This made no difference, and I started to get annoyed – I was eager to get hold of some of that coffee Bill was talking about. 'This is ridiculous,' I said. 'Two fingers on my left hand won't work; stupid things feel numb.' Then my lace worked loose, and I pulled my boots off, throwing them into the back. I should have taken more notice of the numbness at the time, but I didn't. Coffee takes priority over everything.

We started down the rough track. The snow fell in large, lazy flakes, blowing off the windscreen without sticking, and brushing silently past my window. The light was dimming, holding that luminous, ethereal glow of evening that is found only in the mountains. I remembered a card Jan, my long-time friend and fellow traveller, had once sent to me which bore the words, 'In the mountains we forget to count the days.' I realised that this was right: we'd been in Canada for three weeks, and I hadn't the faintest idea what day it was. I made a mental note to check when we got back to the cabin.

We were both silent as I drove, deep in our own thoughts, although I knew those thoughts would be the same. We were due to fly back to the UK in a couple of weeks. Did we stay longer, or did we come back to continue our search another time? Canada was so vast, but we'd narrowed our choice down to Alberta and the Rockies. Was this what we'd continue to do? Return each year in the late autumn or winter, a time special to both of us, still travelling, still searching? But there was one more thing I knew I had to do in the UK. I had to finish The Book. I'd planned to finish it in Canada, but the paperwork, notes and data were too extensive to bring with me, and I'd found that memory wasn't enough.

I snapped back to the present as we got to the brow of a long downward hill, which eventually led to the outskirts of Banff. I pulled over, and gasped at the breathtaking view in front of us. Two lakes lay below, frozen and still, a study in black and silver in the dusk. Then streaks of vermilion and gold lit the sky, and I'd held my breath at such incredible beauty as the last of the day's sun shone briefly between high peaks. The sides of the forest and the images of the mountains were reflected in the lakes, the crimson sky mirrored in their unfrozen centres. There was no way to tell which was earth and which was sky; they were one. And Bill, never emotional, always in control, reached over and held my hand in stunned silence. We stayed like that for a few seconds, breathless, watching the colour recede until only black and white remained.

Bill broke the silence. 'That's why we keep coming back, and that's why eventually we'll stay.' And at that moment I didn't doubt for a moment that it was true. But fate apparently had other ideas.

Six months later I was sitting in a neurologist's office, the numbness in my fingers having turned to a weakness in my arm. 'I think you have the beginning of Parkinson's Disease,' he said. 'That doesn't sound good,' I'd replied, not too sure how else to answer. 'Aren't I a bit young to get something like that?'

'No; you can get it at any age. Some people are unlucky and get it earlier than others. I have two colleagues who go climbing with me, I mean serious climbing, in the Alps: they both have it. Had it for over ten years; doesn't stop them climbing. I certainly wouldn't be climbing with them if I wasn't sure they were both capable and competent.' Well, I thought, if they can climb with Parkinson's, then I can definitely keep walking in Canadian forests with it.

Driving home with Bill we'd discussed the implications. There didn't seem to be a lot wrong with me at the moment. My left hand and arm were definitely weaker than they used to be, and sometimes when I walked I felt a bit off balance, but that was more or less it. We'd both agreed that you could spend a lifetime worrying about the 'what ifs' and the 'I hope nots', but basically life is for living, and we both knew we'd be back in Canada next October. In fact our final joint words on the subject, spoken more or less at the same time, were identical. 'It could have been worse, I could just have been told I had cancer.' That thought reduced the rating of my condition to an absolute zero.

So, early October 2011 we were again heading for the Rockies and the cabin. We didn't have to be back in the UK until mid-December, and were determined to make the most of every second we had out there. Early snows, spectacular walks, snowshoeing and abundant wildlife made it two remarkable and unforgettable months. Elk brushed past the cabin in the early evening, a moose and yearling calf seemed to have become neighbours, mink terrorised squirrels in the trees next to us, and we disturbed deer every time we walked in the woods. We'd seen grizzlies around the cabin before, but were delighted to catch sight of a black bear tearing into an old log one afternoon, bits of bark and snow flying in all directions. Then the following day we were driving along a narrow back road, and a large black wolf had dropped off a snow bank onto the track in front of us, calmly trotting past our vehicle as if we didn't exist. Our response had been a little less calm as we dived for our cameras. A couple of days later, in a heavy snowstorm, we'd driven slowly and cautiously back to the cabin one evening. For a few moments the snow stopped, and just as we crested an icy hill I looked up from the road and instantly yelled at Bill. 'Stop: Bear!' Framed in front of us was a panoramic view of the Bow River valley, and in the distance, barely discernible in the half-light stood a grizzly bear. Magnificent and motionless, he gazed across the river, immobilised in a timeless picture. 'Camera,' Bill stuttered, already having it in his hand: then immediately jumped out of the vehicle into deep snow. But we were too far away, and seconds later the snow returned with a vengeance, forcing Bill back into the warmth.

The following day the mountains looked stunning. Heavy snow blanketed them, and more snow was forecast for late evening. We stood near Sunshine Village above Banff, gazing around at the high peaks. Everywhere was deserted, but in a couple of weeks the ski runs would open, and the stillness would be broken by a riot of skiers and snowboarders arriving to enjoy pristine snow. I looked up in the direction of Goats Eye, Eagle and Lookout Mountains, remembering previous years and previous ski runs. Of all of them, Goats Eye had been my favourite. A movement above, and a golden eagle soared above the summits, one of the last few stragglers on a migratory path that takes place across the Rockies each year. Thinking that the sky really did look bigger in the Rockies, I'd glanced higher, shielding my eyes against a dazzling sun. High cirrus streaks, and just below them the vapour trail of a jet climbing steadily. For no particular reason I shivered: something had changed.

Late December and we were back in the UK, already planning our return to Canada next October. But it's not to be. 'I'm afraid you have cancer,' the consultant in front of me was saying, and I immediately thought back to our words when I found out I had Parkinson's! How weird life was. We walked out of the breast unit contemplating all we'd been told. I'd only found the lump the last month in Canada, so it had been caught early and the prognosis was good. As with all events in our lives, good or bad, Bill and I went searching for coffee. 'It could have been worse,' I said to him. 'They could have told me I had Parkinson's'!

After coffee and at least one sticky cake, we walked back to the car. We'd discussed all there was to discuss, and we both knew Canada was out, for the next year anyway. But there was always the year after: it wasn't going anywhere. As Bill unlocked the car I looked up, and wasn't surprised to see the high vapour trail of a jet crossing the sky. I couldn't help but smile and remember. Then for no apparent reason I thought about a lad I used to work closely with many years ago. Quiet and reserved, with a deep velvety voice, his favourite expression when anything went wrong had always been the same, 'The gods play with us, Susan.' You know what, looking back, I think he was probably right.

Lightning Source UK Ltd.
Milton Keynes UK
UKOW05f0006230114

225119UK00002B/176/P